Introduction

Planet Earth is teeming with life; we share it with at least one million different kinds of animals. Most of the planet is inhabitable. There

are the frozen lands of the Arctic and Antarctic, the cool coniferous forests of the north, wide grasslands, oceanic islands, dry deserts and lush tropical forests. Then there are the oceans themselves and the rivers, lakes and ponds inland.

Whatever the place, there are animals which can thrive there. We say that they have become adapted to their environment. No two animals living in the same place will live in exactly the same way. Some are hunters, others eat plants and some live on other animals as parasites. Each has its own way of living, its own answer to the question, 'How shall I survive?'

This book is about those answers. It is about the adaptations animals have which let them survive. In a way, every

living thing is amazing, because it fits into its world. If it didn't, it wouldn't be here.

Some animals are especially amazing because of the way they feed. Hunters use speed, stealth, strength or camouflage; others resort to traps, poison, even echo-location. The hunted have tricks of their own. Some are dull-coloured to avoid being seen. Others startle their enemies with flash colouring. To get away they glide, swim, leap, 'pronk' or sprint. Some retreat beneath

Andrew Charman

DRAGON'S WORLD

CHILDREN'S BOOKS

DRAGON'S WORLD

CHILDREN'S BOOKS

Dragon's World Ltd
Limpsfield
Surrey RH8 0DY
Great Britain

First published by Dragon's World Ltd, 1996

© Dragon's World Ltd, 1996

British Library
Cataloguing in Publication Data
The catalogue record for this book is available from the British Library.

ISBN 1 85028 312 5

Editor: Diana Briscoe
Text: Andrew Charman
Picture Researcher: Richard Philpott
Designer: Mel Raymond
Art Director: John Strange
Design Assistants: Karen Ferguson
                              Victoria Furbisher
DTP Manager: Michael Burgess
Editorial Director: Pippa Rubinstein

Typeset by Dragon's World Ltd
in Stempel Garamond and Gill

Printed in Italy

Contents

armour; many find safety in groups.

Finding a mate is essential if your kind is to survive and some go to great lengths to attract one. There are birds that make gardens, beetles that glow and mammals that head-butt each other.

Once an animal has found a mate, it must provide for its young. Some build dams, others tunnel into trees. There is one bird who abandons her offspring to other birds to look after, and another who puts her chicks into a prison.

Everywhere you look, there are creatures a person wouldn't dream of making up. My favourite is the frog who looks after his eggs by swallowing them. What's yours?

Andrew Charman

Above: proboscis monkeys.
Below: polar bears.

Opposite
Top left: hummingbird.
Top right: giraffes.
Bottom: fiddler crab.

Ant

SOCIAL INSECTS

Ants are found all over the world. The secret of their success is that they live in very organized groups called colonies – they work together, building a nest in which their eggs and young are safe.

There are different kinds of ant and each has a special job to do. The queen lays the eggs, most of which become females called workers. They build the nest and defend it; they look after the queen, the eggs and the young insects (larvae), and they forage for food. At certain times, male ants and new queens are produced. They have wings and fly away from the nest in a swarm. The males die after mating has taken place. The new queen starts another colony.

The queen is the most important member of the colony. She is the only one who can lay eggs, which means that she is the mother of all the ants in the colony. Workers feed and clean her, and take her eggs to a place where they are cared for.

Some Australian ants use their work-mates as living storage jars. When they collect plenty of nectar – the sweet liquid from flowers – the ants take it in and their bodies become swollen. They hang from the roof of the nest until the food is needed.

▼ Army ants foraging on the forest floor. These ants sometimes march in long columns over the forest floor searching for food. They are always hungry and will attack almost anything, even large mammals.

Different ants eat different kinds of food. Harvester ants store seeds in underground chambers, while leaf-cutter ants carry pieces of leaves underground and use them to grow a fungus. Some ants keep other insects called aphids. They take a sugary substance from the aphids which they use as food, in much the same way that people take milk from cows.

Cockroach

INCREDIBLE SURVIVOR

Most people hate cockroaches and some spend a great deal of time and effort trying to get rid of them. In spite of this, these large insects show no signs of disappearing – they have been on Earth for millions of years and have spread to many parts of the world. Fossils show us that cockroaches were living on Earth more than 300 million years ago.

Wild cockroaches are common in hot countries. With their flat bodies they are able to crawl into cracks and crevices, and they can be difficult to remove completely from a house. They leave their droppings everywhere. There are over 3,500 different kinds of cockroaches. Their markings allow them to blend in with their surroundings.

▲ It is when cockroaches come into our homes that they cause offence. There they find warmth and fragments of food.

Ladybirds taste horrible. They advertise this fact with their red and black markings. Cockroaches, on the other hand, are very tasty to some birds. Some have got over this by imitating the markings of ladybirds. Birds think they will not taste nice and leave them alone.

▼ The cockroaches' long antennae are organs for touching. At night they use them to feel their way about and to find food.

Scarab Beetle

BALL-ROLLING INSECT

There are more than 20,000 different kinds of scarab beetle, and they can be found in every continent except Antarctica. They all eat dung. The most famous scarab beetle comes from Egypt and is 1–2.5 cm long. The largest beetle in the world – the 10-cm long goliath beetle – belongs to the scarab beetle family, as does the rhinoceros beetle.

When a dung beetle finds a pile of dung, it moulds a portion of it into a ball, using its legs, and then rolls it away. The ball is buried and later eaten.

Dung beetles provide food for their young in the same way. A breeding pair will bury a ball of dung, but this time the female moulds the ball into a pear shape and lays her eggs in the 'neck' of the pear. When the young hatch, they eat the dung. By the time it is all gone, they are ready to emerge from the soil as adult beetles.

A pair of dung beetles will sometimes help each other to roll away a ball of dung even if they do not mean to breed.

To the Ancient Egyptians, the scarab beetle was a sacred animal. They believed that a great scarab beetle named Khrostre lived in the sky and turned the world around with its back legs. Thousands of carvings of Khrostre have been excavated by archaeologists working in Egypt.

▼A dung beetle can move a ball of dung larger than itself by rolling it. It places its front legs on the ground, its back legs against the ball and pushes.

Flea

UNWELCOME DINNER GUEST

Fleas are parasites. A parasite gets its food and protection from another living thing (the host) and gives nothing in return. Adult fleas feed on the blood of mammals (including humans) and birds.

They are very well adapted for this lifestyle. The flattened body of the flea allows it to move easily through fur or feathers. It is not harmed by the host's scratching, because the flea's skin is thick and hard.

Fleas are insects, but they do not have wings. They travel from host to host by leaping. Their leaps are extraordinary. Some fleas can jump nearly 200 times their own body length. If a human could

match that, they would be making a jump of about 340 m.

Fleas tend to live on animals that make nests or burrows. This is because their young (larvae) live in the dirt, dust and debris that gathers in such places.

▼ Fleas have evolved special mouth parts for piercing the skin of their victims and sucking up the blood.

When a flea bites, it injects into its victim a special substance which stops the blood from clotting. This is what causes the irritating bump which makes the mammal, bird or human want to scratch.

Glow-worm

LIVING NIGHT-LIGHT

The glow-worm is actually a member of the firefly or lightning beetle family. It got its name because the female lacks wings and looks like a worm. Glow-worms are active in June and July and are found across Europe. They live in hedgerows and grassy meadows, particularly on hillsides.

At night the female climbs out of the crevice in which she has been hiding all day and on to the end of a twig or leaf. Then she dips her head, raises her tail and glows to attract a male. He has large eyes for seeing her and wings for flying to her. Eggs are laid on moss or grass stems and the larvae take three years to grow into adults. The larvae eat snails.

▲ This glow-worm from New Zealand is making a new nest.

Female glow-worms only glow to attract a male and turn out the light if they are disturbed. The young glow-worm is usually unlit, but will glow to frighten away a predator. The light is made when the glow-worm allows oxygen into its special light organs, causing a chemical reaction.

▼ Glow-worms lighting up a cave. Humans can see these lights up to 90 m away. Male glow-worms may be able to see them from even greater distances.

Grasshopper

SINGER IN THE GRASS

Walk through a rough meadow or beside a hedge on a summer's day, and you can hear the grasshopper's chirruping song. This sound is not made with the grasshopper's mouth, but with its legs. Along the larger joint of the long back legs are a series of 'pegs'. The insect rubs these against its wings to make the song. This is called stridulation.

It is usually the male grasshopper who is singing – trying to attract a female. Incidentally, the grasshopper's ears are not on its head, but on the underside of its body. Their close relatives, the crickets, have ears on their knees. After mating, the female lays her eggs in an egg-pod which she buries in the ground to keep it away from enemies.

▲ Lines, patches and small areas of colour help to break up the outline of the grasshopper and make it hard to see. Some are very well-camouflaged.

Each species of grasshopper has its own song. This is important, because different species cannot breed with each other, and the female needs to know that she is listening to a male of the same species as herself.

▼ With its long back legs, the grasshopper can jump out of danger. It can combine this leap with flight.

Mantis

INSECT AMBUSHER

Mantises are patient and deadly, standing motionless waiting for their unwary prey to come within reach. The typical pose is with the front legs raised, making the mantis look as if it is praying. These front legs are made for catching and holding prey. They have rows of spines along them and are hinged in such a way that they can snap together in a movement so fast it is just a blur.

The prey is eaten alive, slowly. Mantises are often quite wasteful with their food, eating just a little and throwing the bulk of it away.

To the female mantis, a male is just another meal, so if he wants to mate with her he must approach her very carefully. He creeps towards her, taking perhaps an hour to move 30 cm. If the female sees the male, or if they are disturbed while they are mating, she will usually eat him, head first.

▼ The mantis's head swivels in all directions, allowing the insect to follow its prey's movements. The large eyes help it to pin-point its victim very accurately.

Mantises are often shaped and coloured to blend in very well with their background. Some resemble dead leaves, others look so like flowers that butterflies and other insects visit them expecting to find nectar, but get a deadly surprise instead.

Stag Beetle

WRESTLING INSECT

Stag beetles get their name from the two large horns on the male's head. These are really much enlarged jaws (up to 2 cm long), not horns. The male uses them to defend his territory against other males. At dusk, the holder takes up a threatening posture on a stone or log.

If this does not scare away the intruder, the two will grapple with each other. Each tries to grab the other around his middle and raise him up. The winner throws his opponent down. If the loser falls on to his back, he will be helpless and at the mercy of ants.

The female has much smaller jaws and can inflict a nasty bite on larger enemies. She lays her eggs in rotting wood. The

larvae eat the wood and take three years to turn into pupae and then to adults.

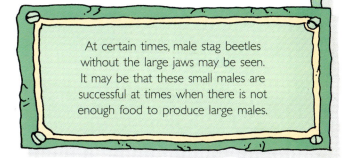

At certain times, male stag beetles without the large jaws may be seen. It may be that these small males are successful at times when there is not enough food to produce large males.

▼ Male stag beetles wrestle to defend their right to breed. Females do not take part in such fighting, and so do not have the much-enlarged jaws.

Stick Insect

MASTERS OF DISGUISE

Stick insects move about and feed on plants at night. During the day, they stay completely still and cannot be seen by predators, because they look exactly like twigs. Most stick insects can be found in the tropical forests of eastern Asia. They vary in size: the largest is over 30.5 cm long and is the largest insect on Earth.

Most stick insects do not have wings. Some of those that do have brightly coloured wings. When disturbed, the sudden flash of colour as the insect takes off confuses the predator. The colour vanishes just as suddenly when the insect lands and refolds its wings. This is called 'flash coloration', and is a method of escape used by many insects.

▶ Stick insects are so well-disguised. that they can only be seen when they move.

▼ Stick insects mating.

Stick insects lay large eggs, which look like seeds. Sometimes they look just like the seeds of the tree or bush on which the insect feeds. One North American stick insect lays so many eggs that their falling sounds just like rain.

Termite

INSECT ARCHITECTS

There are 1,700 different kinds of termite. They are social insects living in colonies, like ants. They live in huge nests, or mounds, made of sand and droppings mixed with saliva into a cement. The shape of the nest depends on the kind of termite that makes it. Tunnels to the outside are opened and closed by the insects to control the temperature inside the nest.

The most important members of the colony are the king and queen. The queen's body is hugely swollen by the eggs she carries. Both she and the king, who fertilizes her eggs, once flew from another colony, but then lost their wings.

▲ Termite nests or mounds can be up to 6 m high and are incredibly strong. People trying to remove them from building sites sometimes have to use explosives.

▼ Inside a special chamber in the termite nest is the queen. She does nothing but lay eggs, and is fed and cleaned by workers and guarded by soldiers. The soldiers have large jaws for biting enemies.

Compass termites from northern Australia build tall wedge-shaped nests up to 3.5 m high. The wider, flat sides point to the east and west. This may be a way of controlling the nest's temperature. The flat sides receive warmth from the Sun in the morning and evening, but not the dangerously hot midday sun.

Weaving Ant

INSECT TAILORS

Weaving ants live at the edges of forests in south-eastern Asia and tropical Australia. They do not make their nests in the ground as do many kinds of ants, but use the leaves high in the trees.

Worker ants bring together the edges of two leaves still attached to the tree, by holding one in their jaws and the other with their feet. Another worker then binds the leaves together with silk. The silk is not produced by the adult insects, but by the larvae. A larva is held in the jaws of the sewing worker and

▲ These weaver ants from Indonesia are making a nest by binding together the edges of a living leaf with silk.

Weaving ants sometimes play host to the caterpillar of the moth-butterfly. This is not a good deal for the ants. The caterpillar eats their young, but the ants cannot attack the intruder because it is protected by a horny, oval-shaped shield.

gently squeezed to produce its silk.

These ants often live with a guest – the caterpillar of the common oak blue butterfly. The caterpillar releases a sweet, sugary liquid and other substances on which the ants like to feed. In return, the ants protect the caterpillar from hungry wasps or spiders. At night the ants make it a shelter of leaves, and during the day they swarm over it, ready to attack any intruder.

◀ Building the nest, like so many activities in an ant colony, is a group effort.

Bee

HONEY MAKER

There are many different kinds of bees. Some live in groups of a dozen or so, others live alone. The most social of all are the honeybees. There may be up to 80,000 honeybees in a single nest.

The central feature of the nest is the cell, many of which are joined together to form a comb. Each cell is hexagonal (six-sided). This is a strong shape and it uses up less wax and energy to build than would other shapes.

Some of the cells are used to store food in the form of pollen and nectar, which the bees gather from flowers. The nectar will turn to honey inside the cells. All the eggs are laid by the queen. She drops one into each cell and they are then tended by the female worker bees.

▲ Each cell is made of wax which comes from the bees' bodies. They knead the wax with their mouth parts and front legs to make it soft and workable.

Each cell in a honeycomb has walls of the same thickness. The worker bees involved in building the honeycomb can tell the thickness of a wall by prodding it with their antennae and seeing how much it 'gives'.

▼ As a worker bee moves from flower to flower, it stores the pollen it has collected in the pollen baskets on its hind legs.

Monarch Butterfly

WANDERING INSECT

The monarch is the only migratory butterfly that goes on a specific journey every year and returns the next. Those that live in North America spend the summer in southern Canada and the northern part of the USA. In the autumn, they gather in groups and fly south.

As they fly, others join them until they form a 'flock' of thousands. At their destination, which may be Mexico, Florida in the east or California in the west, they gather in trees and hibernate for the rest of the winter. Some may have flown well over 3,200 km.

The following spring, the butterflies fly north again, laying their eggs along the way. It may be June before they are back in the north and by this time they will have passed through several generations. Those that finally arrive in the north will be the grandchildren or great-grandchildren of those who flew south the previous autumn.

▲ A monarch butterfly resting and feeding on nectar from a buddleia plant. This bush is so popular with moths and butterflies that it is sometimes called the 'Butterfly Bush'.

▼ These monarch butterflies have flown from the forest and are warming themselves in the sun, perhaps before beginning a long journey.

The caterpillars (young form) of monarch butterflies feed on poisonous plants. The poison does not harm them, but it makes them unpleasant to eat. The poison stays in their bodies, and so the adults' bold colours are a warning to predators.

Ladybird

INSECT FAVOURITE

The ladybird has always been one of our favourite insects, even before scientists knew how useful it was. There are many different kinds, but usually they are red or yellow with black spots, although some are black with red spots. All ladybirds have one great advantage over other insects: they taste horrible and their bright colours warn birds and other predators of this fact.

Ladybirds lay their eggs on the underside of leaves, often on plants infested with aphids, for these little insects are the ladybirds' food. Young ladybirds eat huge numbers of aphids (which damage the plants they live on by sucking their sap) and so they are useful to farmers and gardeners.

▲ Three seven-spot ladybirds. The number of spots on a ladybird tells you which species you are looking at, not how old it is.

In summer, ladybirds fly about among the leaves. In the winter they hibernate, often in groups of up to a hundred, under loose bark or on the sheltered side of a post.

▼ These ladybirds from North America are gathering on a bush before hibernating for the winter.

Atlas Moth

CHEMICAL DETECTOR

If they are to have young, all animals must find a mate. This is quite easy for animals that live in colonies or groups, but it is not so simple for those who spend most of their time alone. Moths have solved this problem in their own particular way and the atlas moth is a good example.

When they wish to attract a mate, female atlas moths give off chemical signals called 'pheromones'. These cannot be detected by other animals, but the male atlas moths have some special sense organs on their heads for picking up the signals: their antennae. The large and feathery antennae of the male atlas

moth are very sensitive; they have up to 10,000 receptors. With these it is able to pick up the chemical signals given off by a female who is up to 1.5 km away.

Crabs, barnacles, spiders and many other insects produce pheromones to attract their mates. Ants use them to lay trails, while some mammals use them to mark their territories.

▼ The atlas moth is one of the largest moths in the world. The females are larger than the males and may have a wingspan of up to 25 cm.

Moths are mostly nocturnal, which means that they are active at night. They cannot use sight to find each other, so that is why they use chemical signals. However, light attracts them which is why you often find moths on windows or flying around lamps in the evening.

Silk Moth

CLOTH-MAKING MOTHS

The cloth we call silk does not come from a plant as with cotton, or from the fur of a mammal as is the case with wool. It comes from the caterpillars of silk moths. The caterpillars hatch from eggs after the winter and begin to eat. They eat mulberry leaves, and have such big appetites that by the time they are fully grown (about 42 days later) they will be 10,000 times heavier than when they hatched.

The caterpillars then make their cocoons. They stop feeding and start producing a thread of silk which they bind around themselves. Eventually, each pupa, as it is now known, is enclosed inside a ball of silk. It then begins to metamorphose (change) into an adult moth.

▼ Silk moths are the only insects that are controlled wholly by humans – there are none in the wild. They have well-developed wings, but cannot fly.

The silk that makes the cocoon is one continuous thread about 305 m long. It can be unwound on to reels and woven into cloth. The silk industry began in China in 2140 BC, and was kept a secret for 2,000 years. It is said that the secret came to the West when two monks smuggled some silk moth eggs to Constantinople (now Istanbul in Turkey) in a tube of bamboo.

Hunting Wasp

PARENT PROVIDERS

Wasps come in two basic types: social (wasps that live together in a colony), and solitary (those living alone). Hunting wasps belong to the second group. The potter wasp is a good example.

After mating, the female potter wasp makes a little pot out of wet mud. Then she goes hunting. She does not kill her prey, but paralyzes it (or makes it helpless) with her sting and puts it into the pot. She lays an egg alongside it and seals the opening with a lump of mud.

Inside the pot, the wasp larva finds itself provided with a fresh supply of food. When the food has all gone, the larva is ready to pupate, that is, to undergo a complete body change and turn into an adult wasp.

▲ Inside the nest made by the hunting wasp is the wasp's egg and a store of caterpillars to feed the young when it emerges.

It is an advantage that the insect food is paralyzed rather than killed. If it were dead, it would begin to decay and the larva would not be able to eat it and so die. The larva sucks the juices from the living insect in such a way that it stays alive until it is almost completely eaten.

▼ This female hunting wasp has caught a caterpillar and is about to drag it into her nest.

Earthworm

WILD GARDENERS

We are so familiar with earthworms that we tend to forget how important they are. As they eat, they help to break down plant material so that the nutrients, or goodness, in the material goes into the soil. Their constant burrowing in the ground allows air to circulate and rainwater to drain properly. Without earthworms, the soil would soon become hard and lifeless.

Earthworms make burrows by pushing aside the soil or by swallowing it as food. Some kinds bring this swallowed soil to the surface and excrete

▲ An earthworm's body is made up of segments. The broad band on its body is called the saddle or clitellum. After mating, this produces the cocoon which contains the eggs.

it as little mounds, or worm casts. Worms also feed by stretching out of their burrows and dragging bits of plants underground.

In the course of a year, the worms in a half hectare of grassland can bring from seven to eighteen tonnes of soil to the surface. In this way, they till, or turn, the soil.

Earthworms have no eyes or ears, but their bodies are very sensitive to vibrations. They often flee to the surface when they feel the movements of an enemy, such as a mole, digging nearby. If a worm loses part of its body, it has the ability to regrow the part that has gone. New segments grow at the front and rear ends of the body.

◀ An earthworm pulling a leaf down into its burrow so that it can eat it undisturbed by predators.

Scorpion

DESERT STINGER

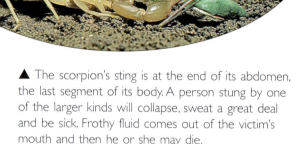

Scorpions are found in all the warm parts of the world, particularly in deserts. They hide during the day under a rock or a log. Those who stray into houses hide under carpets, in beds and shoes. This can be dangerous: some kinds, particularly the 20-cm African scorpion, have a sting that is fatal to humans.

A scorpion usually catches its prey, mostly spiders and insects, with its two large and powerful claws. The sting is only used if the victim struggles. Scorpions live alone and are aggressive towards each other, so mating requires a male to approach a female carefully.

▼ Young scorpions are born one or two at a time, over a period of several weeks. In the early days, these perfect miniature scorpions ride on their mother's back. After seven days, they are large enough to live on their own.

▲ The scorpion's sting is at the end of its abdomen, the last segment of its body. A person stung by one of the larger kinds will collapse, sweat a great deal and be sick. Frothy fluid comes out of the victim's mouth and then he or she may die.

Some kinds of scorpions 'sing' like grasshoppers by rubbing one part of their body against another. The sound, however, has a different purpose. It is not used to attract a mate, but to warn an intruder that the scorpion has a dangerous sting.

Snail

ONE-FOOTED CRAWLER

Snails are found in many gardens, and are most common in places that have chalky soils. This is because their shells are made of the same substance as chalk. They look shiny because they have a glaze of protein.

Snails move along with waves of their muscular body, which is actually a kind of foot. Their journey over the rough ground is made more comfortable by a trail of slime. There is another yellowy slime produced if the snail is attacked.

Each snail has both male and female sex organs and when two snails are mating both will receive sperm. The eggs are laid in holes in the soil and covered over. They hatch in two to four weeks and the young have their own small shells. As the snail grows, new chalk is added to the shell around the lip of the opening to make the shell larger.

▲ A Roman snail. The snail's head has two pairs of tentacles. The larger of the two pairs has the eyes at the tips and is pushed inside-out when the snail emerges from its shell.

Snails have a strong homing instinct. After a night of foraging, they will often return to the same place to hide during the day. This hideout may be shared with other snails.

▼ Inside the snail's mouth is a file-like tongue with 15,000 horny teeth arranged in rows. The animal uses these to eat leaves, including those of stinging nettles and holly trees.

Spider

WEB BUILDERS

'Orb spider' is the name given to the many different species that build orb- or wheel-shaped webs. Spiders produce silk threads from organs called 'spinnerets' on the underside of their bodies. The spider makes an oblong-shaped frame, and then adds threads which spread out from the middle like wheel spokes.

A spiral is laid on to this, going from the middle to the outer edge. Another spiral is then spun going the other way. This one is sticky and, as it is laid down, the spider cuts away the earlier spiral. Then the spider hides and waits. It feels for vibrations on the threads which tell it that an insect has been caught. Then it rushes out, wraps the struggling victim in silk and paralyzes it with poison.

▲ A white lady spider from the Sahara desert showing the sharp pedipalps (jaws) it uses for catching and stunning its prey.

Some of the larger kinds of orb spiders, which live in tropical countries, catch birds and bats as well as insects. Their webs are made of strong, thick silk and can be up to 2.5 m across. People gather these on to looped sticks and use them as fishing nets.

▼ This garden spider's web can be seen because dew has formed on the threads. The main picture shows a frog-eating spider with its latest victim.

Trap-door Spider

EIGHT-LEGGED ENGINEERS

Trap-door spiders do not make a web in which to catch insects. Instead, they dig a pit in the ground and line it with silk. When the work is done, the pit may be 30 cm deep and up to 4 cm wide. It is then fitted with a solid, round trap-door made of layers of soil and silk and a hinge of silk. The outside is decorated with moss and other plant material so it is almost impossible to see.

The spiders hunt at night. Each one lays silken trip threads around the outside of its pit and then waits just inside the half-open door with its legs touching the threads. When an insect walks across them, the spider feels the movement, rushes out, grabs the insect and drags it into the pit.

▲ A Malaysian trap-door spider emerging from its pit. The lid of the trap is over its back.

▼ A trap-door spider waiting for an insect to wander by. Inside its pit, the spider is safe from rain, fierce heat and predators, such as hunting wasps.

Some trap-door spiders make their lids in such a way that they are a perfect fit. There are teeth on the lid which slot into grooves on the side of the pit. In the walls of the pit are two holes. Should a predator try to expose the spider, it can secure its feet in these holes and hold the lid down.

Fiddler Crab

BEACH WAVERS

The male fiddler crab has one extremely large claw and one of normal size. He uses his small claw for picking up small animals from the mud and passing them to his mouth. The large claw is used for displays to other fiddler crabs.

These crabs live on tropical beaches. When the tide goes out, they scamper out of their burrows and wave their claws at each other. Some hold up the claw like a shield, some wave, others throw up both claws as if in surprise. The display means: 'This is my patch of sand. Keep away.' Some fiddler crabs will make a chirruping sound like a grasshopper if another crab tries to enter its burrow. It makes the sound by rubbing a claw against its shell.

▼ If one fiddler crab enters the territory of another, they will fight. Each uses its large claw to try to throw the other on to its back.

▲ Only male fiddler crabs have the much-enlarged claw. It is used for displaying to or fighting with other males.

When the tide returns, each crab cuts a disk of mud and carries it back to its burrow. It goes inside, lowering the disk in place as a lid. A bubble of air is trapped inside and the crab breathes this until the water recedes again.

Arrow-poison Frog

LETHAL AMPHIBIAN

Many amphibians have poison in their bodies or can give out or secrete it from their skins, but few are as lethal as the arrow-poison frogs of Central and South America. For centuries, the poison in their bodies has been used by the native peoples of the Amazon rainforests to make their hunting arrows more deadly.

Many arrow-poison frogs are brightly coloured, frequently with red, yellow or black markings. These colours are often used in the animal world as a warning to other animals that they are nasty to eat. The colours make the frogs stand out – they do not need to hide from enemies as attackers stay away from them. The most lethal poison comes from the kokoi frog of Columbia, South America. Just 0.0003 g is enough to kill a person.

▲ Some arrow-poison frogs live on the forest floor. These two, from Central America, live among the trees and feed on insects.

Golden arrow-poison frogs are unusual in that the male and female play together before mating. They spend 2–3 hours jumping at each other before the female finally lays her eggs and the male fertilizes them. The male carries the eggs on his back, which is where they hatch and grow.

▼ Arrow-poison frogs can be identified by their bright colours and by the nail-like plate on each toe.

Darwin's Frog

MOUTH-BREEDING FROG

This little frog lives in southern-most parts of South America, where it hops about among the trees. It has a very unusual way of looking after its young.

During the breeding season, the female lays 20–30 eggs. The male stands over them until the tadpoles are about to hatch, then he scoops them up with his tongue and swallows them. They go into his vocal sac – a large pouch under his throat and belly, which he uses to make his small, bell-like call. He keeps the young tadpoles there while they grow.

When the tadpoles are about 1 cm long, and only have a stump of a tail left, he opens his mouth and out they jump. It is very unusual for the male to carry the young as they grow.

▲ Inside the male frog's vocal sac, each tadpole lives on the yoke that was part of its original egg. This male has just released a froglet from his vocal sac.

▼ While the tadpoles are inside his vocal sac, the male Darwin's frog can continue to eat. This male and his froglet are from Chile in South America.

Male Darwin's frogs do not necessarily carry their own tadpoles. Several females will lay their eggs together in a mass and the males will pick up those that are nearest to them.

Flying Frog

TREE LEAPER

The flying frog lives in trees. At night, it looks for grasshoppers to eat. It can hop over 2 m between branches, but if the next tree looks more inviting, it can reach that, too. The frog launches itself into the air, spreads out its webbed toes and glides. It also curves the underside of its body. This gives it extra lift, and it can travel up to 15 m.

This tree frog does not lay its eggs in pools of water, but among the leaves of trees. The eggs are laid along with a substance called albumen. The adults beat this into a frothy mass, which then hardens on the outside. Inside it stays moist. The eggs, and later the tadpoles, stay protected inside until the rains come and wash them into pools below.

▲ A flying frog from the forests of Asia. In a glide, the toes are fully stretched. The length and direction of the glide can be controlled to some extent.

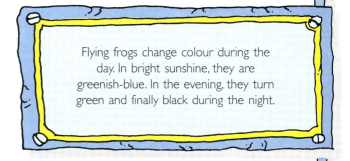

Flying frogs change colour during the day. In bright sunshine, they are greenish-blue. In the evening, they turn green and finally black during the night.

▼ This flying frog comes from Malaysia. At the end of a glide, each foot acts like a little parachute, slowing the frog's descent.

Basilisk Lizard

WATER RUNNER

Many animals escape from their enemies by simply running away. The basilisk lizard does this, but in a unique way. It lives in Central and South America and spends most of its time in shrubs and trees near to water. The lizard's back legs are shaped like those of a frog. They end in long toes fringed with scales. The feet are not webbed, but they do have large soles.

When alarmed, the basilisk lizard stands up on its back legs and runs, holding its tail out behind it for balance. It can run along the ground or branches in this way but, more unusually, it can run across water, too. If the lizard is moving fast enough, its feet do not break through the surface film of the water. As the lizard slows down, though, it falls into the water and swims away. By then, it is probably safe from harm.

▲ Basilisk lizards are 61 cm long. They have a crest on the head, back and tail. The lizard uses its long tail for balance when it is running along.

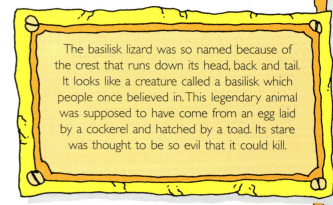

The basilisk lizard was so named because of the crest that runs down its head, back and tail. It looks like a creature called a basilisk which people once believed in. This legendary animal was supposed to have come from an egg laid by a cockerel and hatched by a toad. Its stare was thought to be so evil that it could kill.

◀ The basilisk lizard can run short distances across water to escape from danger. This picture is taken from underwater, so the soles of its feet can be seen.

Boa Constrictor

SNAKES THAT SQUEEZE

There are many stories of people being crushed to death in the coils of huge boa constrictors. Few, if any, of them are true. Boas are large snakes, but they are generally harmless to people. The largest (anacondas) grow to about 4.5 m long, and if one came near, you could escape by simply running away. Smaller animals, such as lizards, birds and rats, have more reason to be fearful. Boas come from Central and South America.

A boa lies in wait for a victim or creeps up on it slowly. It kills not by crushing, which is squeezing the victim's body until it is injured, but by constriction. It constricts by throwing its body around the victim in a series of loops. Each time the victim breaths out, the loops tighten until the animal is suffocated to death. The animal is then swallowed whole. Boas do not kill often. They can survive for several weeks on one meal and spend most of their time resting (conserving energy).

▲ Boas usually lie quietly in wait for their victims.

Boas and many other snakes have special heat-sensitive organs, called 'pits', on their heads. They can detect the heat given off by a warm-blooded animal nearby. This helps them to catch their food more easily, even in the dark.

▲ Boa constrictors do not chew their food; they swallow it whole. They can do this because their jaws come apart easily, allowing large animals to pass between them.

Chameleon

LIZARDS THAT 'SHOOT' THEIR FOOD

Chameleons are a family of lizards found in Africa and Madagascar. The chameleon's tail is held in a tight coil and can be wrapped around a branch for extra grip. The feet also have a strong grip. For much of the time, the lizard sits completely still, waiting for insects and other small animals to come within its reach.

The chameleon is known for its ability to change colour and so blend in with its background. In fact, it cannot alter its colour drastically, but it can change its shade in response to changes in the light. It can also change to show how it feels: an angry chameleon turns dark, a frightened one becomes paler.

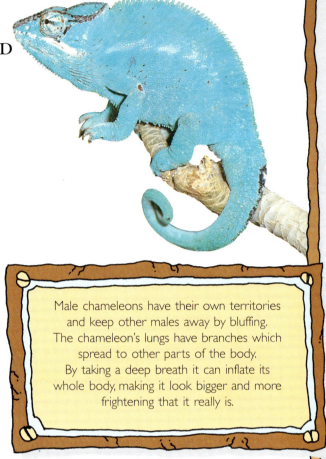

Male chameleons have their own territories and keep other males away by bluffing. The chameleon's lungs have branches which spread to other parts of the body. By taking a deep breath it can inflate its whole body, making it look bigger and more frightening that it really is.

▼ The chameleon catches its prey by shooting out its tongue, which is longer than its head and body combined. In the blink of an eye, the sticky tongue grasps the victim and carries it to the mouth.

Cobra

POISON SPITTER

Poisonous snakes use their poison to kill their prey, such as rats, birds and toads. They do not hunt humans because we are too large. People are bitten by snakes because they tread on them or disturb them. The poison, or venom, is produced by glands in the upper jaw. It travels along ducts to the fangs. When the snake strikes, the fangs pierce the skin and the venom is injected. After the strike, the snake can cling on and 'chew', delivering yet more poison.

The cobra's venom acts on the victim's nervous system. The animal is unable to move, may have difficulty breathing and then its heart stops. This can happen within fifteen minutes of being bitten.

▼ There are several kinds of cobra. They all have hoods on their necks which fan out when they are frightened or excited. This makes the snake look larger and more threatening.

▲ Spitting cobras do not need to strike their victims, instead they spit their venom. They aim for the face and are very accurate at distances of up to 3.5 m.

The king cobra is the largest poisonous snake in the world. They can grow to a length of 5.5 m. A small amount of its venom could kill thirty people.

Crocodile

ANCIENT REPTILE

Hundreds of millions of years ago, the ancestors of today's crocodiles and alligators were living alongside the dinosaurs. These ancient reptiles have hardly changed since then.

Crocodiles live in the warmer parts of the world, and they usually stay close to water. Much of their time is spent basking in the sunshine to stay warm. Sunbathing crocodiles are not interested in food, and it is possible for birds to come close and pick bits of food from their teeth.

Swimming crocodiles float low in the water with just their nostrils and eyes showing. They swallow stones which lodge in their stomachs and help them to stay upright in the water – without them they might roll over.

Crocodiles lay their eggs in pits in the ground or in mounds of leaves. When the young crocodiles are ready to hatch out, they make grunting noises. This is a signal to the mother that she should uncover the eggs.

▲ Nile crocodiles live in lairs dug out of river banks. They feed on fish and land animals.

Crocodiles are cannibals – they will eat each other. Groups of crocodiles tend to be made up of individuals that are the same size. The groups of small crocodiles keep away from the large crocodiles in case they are eaten.

▼ Crocodiles hunt by creeping up on their victims or by lying in wait to ambush them. Animals are caught with a sideways snap of the jaws or knocked down by a blow from the head. They are then dragged under water and drowned.

Frilled Lizard

DESERT BLUFFER

Frilled lizards are found in northern Australia in areas that are sandy and dry. They are about 1 m long with slender, pale brown bodies. Around their necks they have a large frill which normally lies folded over the shoulders.

The lizards rest in trees, coming down to the ground to feed on such animals as ants, spiders and small mammals. If one should be disturbed while it is feeding, it will rear up on its back legs and sprint away, holding its tail out for balance.

If cornered, the lizard will turn and raise the frill on its neck. The frill has ribs in it like those of an umbrella, and when fully opened it can measure 20 cm

▲ The frilled lizard with its frill in its normal position.

or more across. When its frill is raised, the lizard will then sway from side to side with its mouth open. This is a warning display; it means, 'Keep away.'

The frilled lizard is not a dangerous animal, so its warning display is mostly bluff – it is very good at startling or frightening an attacker into retreat.

◀ When alarmed, the frilled lizard extends its frill. This makes the animal look bigger than it really is.

Gecko

WALL-CLIMBING LIZARD

There are many different kinds of geckos – the largest grows to about 35 cm, the smallest to about 3 cm. They live in warm countries all over the world, and can be seen in trees or among rocks.

Geckos are harmless to people, and some kinds have taken to living in houses. They are happiest in places where there are crevices in which they can hide and lights which attract their main food: insects.

To catch these insects, geckos are able to walk up walls and across ceilings. They can even walk on the glass of a window, because of scales and tiny hooks on the undersides of their toes.

▲ Geckos can walk on glass, because of scales and tiny hooks on the undersides of their toes. These give them an amazing grip.

Like many other types of lizards, geckos can shed their tails when attacked by a predator. In time, a new tail will grow to take the place of the lost tail.
Sometimes the tail is not shed completely – in this case the tail heals while another one grows and the gecko then has two tails.

▼ Geckos that are active at night have eyes like those of cats – their pupils are slit-like. These pupils can contract, or become smaller, if exposed to bright light.

Gila Monster

POISONOUS LIZARD

People once believed that the gila monster was impossible to kill and that it had magical powers. This is not true, but it is remarkable for different reasons.

Only two of the 3,000 different species of lizard are poisonous. The gila monster delivers its poison through its teeth. It has a very strong bite and will cling on with a vice-like grip. The poison can cause swelling and sickness, but cannot kill a person unless they are bitten over and over again.

The gila monster does not use its poison to kill its food. It moves slowly and tends to eat things that cannot run away, like eggs and very young animals.

▲ Gila monsters live in the deserts of south-western USA and nearby parts of Mexico. They can grow up to 60 cm long.

When active, the gila monster eats a lot and stores what it does not need as fat in its body, especially in the tail. It can survive a long time on the fat it has stored in its body. One was once recorded to have gone for three years without eating.

▼ When it is searching for food, the gila monster tastes the air with its tongue. The tongue carries scent to a special taste-smell organ in the roof of its mouth. This one is not tasting, but threatening.

Komodo Dragon

LARGEST LIVING LIZARD

Komodo dragons can be found on a few small Indonesian islands, the largest island of which is only 32 by 19 km in size. These are the second largest lizards that have ever lived on Earth (only the sea-living mesosaurs that existed over eleven million years ago were larger). Adult males are about 3 m long and weigh around 136 kg.

Komodo dragons live in caves or in holes among rocks or roots. Each morning they emerge and look for food. Their forked tongues can taste the air and are flicked in and out constantly. Usually, they are trying to find animals that are already dead, but they can also kill pigs, goats and deer. They have also attacked lone children.

The older and larger dragons eat first, keeping the young ones away from the food with swipes from their powerful tails. Komodo dragons gorge themselves on their food. They eat as much as they can and then have to rest for up to a week while they digest their meal.

▲ In the past, Komodo dragons have been hunted for their skins and for zoos. They are now protected in a national park on the island of Komodo.

For centuries, the island of Komodo was uninhabited by humans. Then the Sultan of Sumbawa began to send criminals there as a punishment. They sent back alarming reports of huge lizards which at first were not believed. The first scientific report was not published until 1912.

▼ As with many lizards, the Komodo dragon's tongue is an organ for tasting and smelling. It is flicked in and out, testing the air for the smell of dead meat.

Moloch

THORNY LIZARD

The moloch resembles a walking rosebush stem – its body is covered with spikes. Moloch mealtimes are long affairs, for the lizard eats only ants and it flicks them up with its tongue one at a time. It can pick up thirty to forty-five ants in a minute, and may take 1,000–5,000 in one sitting. It is fortunate that it can live on one good meal for a long time.

After mating, the female moloch digs a 60-cm long tunnel in a bank or mound, and lays her eggs at the end of it. She fills in the tunnel and levels the ground so that a passing predator would have no idea it was there. Later, the young lizards dig their way out and must fend for themselves.

▲ The moloch looks dangerous, but in fact it is quite harmless. It lives in the deserts and other very dry parts of Australia.

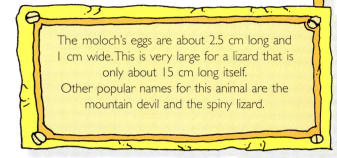

The moloch's eggs are about 2.5 cm long and 1 cm wide. This is very large for a lizard that is only about 15 cm long itself.
Other popular names for this animal are the mountain devil and the spiny lizard.

▼ The moloch is not poisonous or much of a biter, but it presents a mass of sharp spikes to any would-be predator.

Sidewinder

DESERT SNAKE

The sidewinder lives in deserts, in places where there is loose, wind-blown sand and it moves over the sand in an unusual sideways looping movement.

The sidewinder hunts in the early part of the night. It eats rodents, such as kangaroo rats and deer mice. During the day, it rests in mouse-holes or lies buried under a bush, level with the surface of the sand. It can be hard to see.

Like other rattlesnakes, the sidewinder has a rattle at the end of its tail. This is made up of a series of dried scales which were once part of the living skin of the snake. The snake shakes this rattle as a warning to intruders that it has a poisonous bite.

▲ The sidewinder moves over the sand with an unusual sideways looping motion. This lets it grip the loose sand and move rapidly along in search of shelter or prey.

Each time the snake sheds its skin, which it does in order to grow, a scale is left behind and is added to the rattle. As the snake moves about, scales are lost or worn away. Wild snakes rarely have more than fourteen pieces in the rattle, but snakes in a zoo's collection may have up to twenty-nine.

◀ As a sidewinder moves over the desert floor it leaves a characteristic trail of lines.

Giant Tortoise

ARMOURED TANKS

Tortoises are well known for their long lives and slow movements. The most reliable record tells of one which was at least 152 years old. Perhaps it is their slow way of life that lets them live so long. A tortoise in a hurry can trot along at around 3 kph over short distances. Their speed depends on the temperature. They enjoy warm weather and move very little in cold weather.

Tortoises are protected from predators by a bony shell covered with horn. This makes them the most heavily armoured animals alive today. If danger threatens, a tortoise will withdraw its head completely and tuck its legs under the shell. This will deter most attackers.

There were once many giant tortoises on the Galápagos Islands in the Pacific Ocean, but now there are just a few left. Thousands were once caught by sailors to provide meat for their long sea voyages.

▼ Tortoises like to browse on the leaves and flowers of low-growing plants and fruits that fall from trees. These are drinking from a pool on Isabela Island.

Bird of Paradise

FEATHERED SHOW-OFF

When these birds were first brought to Europe nearly 500 years ago, people were dazzled by the beauty of their feathers. They believed the birds had come from paradise. In fact, they come from the forests of New Guinea and Australia. In most species, only the male has the amazing plumage and he uses it to attract a female.

During the breeding season, he selects a branch in full view of several females and displays by flapping his wings or turning upside-down, so that the feathers flop over in a brilliant cascade. Those with fantastically coloured tails fly back and forth. If a female likes what she sees, she will mate with the male. But after that she goes off to lay her eggs and raise her young alone.

▼ The male Raggiana's bird of paradise begins his display in the early morning or afternoon. He hops sideways along a branch with his wings open, then he leans over so that his feathers tumble forwards.

For centuries, the people of Papua New Guinea have used the feathers of birds of paradise in their ceremonial headdresses. When people started selling feathers abroad, too many birds were killed and they became endangered.

Bower-bird

ARTISTIC BIRDS

The satin bower-bird lives in the forests along the coast of eastern Australia. The male is black, but his feathers turn a shimmering blue in sunlight. The female is quite different. Her plumage is pale green and yellow.

The male bird makes a great effort to attract a female. He builds a bower – a tunnel or short avenue – out of twigs and decorates the area around it with small objects, such as snail shells, feathers, flowers and fungi. He chooses things that are the same colour as the female. If human dwellings are near by, he will find pieces of glass, bottle tops, paper and rags to add to his display. He will steal from and try to destroy the nests of other bower birds. When the bower is finished, he brings the female to see it.

If the female is impressed with the bower, she will mate with the male. What appeals to her is not only the number of objects the male has used, but how unusual they are. Strangely it is the female who then goes on to build a nest – the male plays no part in this – in which she rears one to three chicks.

There are several different species of bower-bird. Some build wigwam-shaped shelters. Sometimes these have what looks like a garden around them, bounded by a hedge of twigs and decorated with coloured objects.

▼ The male bower-bird brings the female to his bower. Then he holds some of the decorative objects in his bill and dances for her.

Crane

ELEGANT DANCER

Cranes are elegant long-legged birds. There are fourteen different kinds and the largest stands 1.5 m tall and has a wingspan of 2.3 m. They can be told apart by the markings on their heads and necks. One of the most striking is the crowned crane with its plume of orange-brown feathers resembling a Roman helmet.

Cranes are famous for their dances, which occur throughout the year, but especially during the breeding season. They walk around each other with wings half open, bowing and stretching. Then they leap into the air, as high as 4.5 m, and float slowly to the ground again. In Australia, brolga cranes dance in rows of up to twenty to thirty birds.

▲ This crowned crane is displaying his superb crest of feathers.

One of the unique features of the crane is its long windpipe, which may be 1.5 m long. Half of it is coiled inside the bird's chest and its great length enables the bird to make a loud trombone-like call, which can be heard over long distances. The call serves as an alarm, a greeting, or just a way of making contact with other cranes.

▼ It is not only mating pairs of cranes who dance – often whole groups join in, including young birds who are too young to breed.

Cuckoo

NEST INVADER

In Europe, the cuckoo's call is a sign that spring has arrived. The cuckoo spends the winter in Africa and returns in March as the weather in Europe gets warmer. After mating, the female cuckoo is ready to lay her eggs, but she does not make a nest of her own.

She visits the nests of other, smaller birds, such as robins or warblers. She removes one of their eggs and replaces it with one of her own. Her eggs are small for a bird of her size and the markings on them match very closely those of the other bird. If they did not, the other bird would reject them. The young cuckoo hatches out earlier than the other eggs, and immediately heaves them out of the nest. It has to do this, because it will soon be very large and will need all the food its foster mother can find.

▲ Cuckoos return to Europe in the spring and perch on posts, branches and wires to call for mates. The bird gets its name from its call: an easily recognizable 'cuckoo'.

The cuckoo lays her egg in the foster bird's nest while the other bird is out of sight. She has to do this quickly. Her eggs have extra thick shells so that they do not break as they drop into the nest.

◄ A young cuckoo being fed by its foster parent: a much smaller reed warbler. The cuckoo needs as much food as the original three or four chicks would have wanted.

Woodpecker Finch

TOOL-USING BIRD

On the Galápagos Islands in the Pacific Ocean there are fourteen different kinds of finch. Their bodies are very much alike, but their bills are not the same – they eat different kinds of food. There are ground-feeding seed-eaters, plant-eaters, cactus-eaters and insect-eaters.

One of these finches is called the woodpecker finch. It has a short, strong beak. It uses this to peck into the tunnels made by young insects in trees and cacti. Then it takes a thin twig or cactus spine in its beak and uses it to poke the insects out of their home. This is one of the rare examples of animals using tools. Woodpecker finches have been seen making little piles of cactus spines – a store of tools for future use.

▲ A woodpecker finch pulls an insect grub from a hole in a tree trunk,

▼ The woodpecker finch lacks the long tongue of the true woodpeckers. Instead, it uses a stick to poke insect larvae out of holes in trees and cacti.

It is thought that all these finches descended from just one species that once flew in from the USA. Over a long period of time, they have changed to suit different ways of life. This process is called evolution.

Frigate Bird

PIRATES OF THE SEA

Frigate birds are expert fliers, living near the coasts of warm seas. The largest have wingspans of 2 m, but they have weak legs and are not good perchers. They use their long wings to soar on the lightest breezes, swoop with great speed, hover effortlessly and turn with amazing agility. In the breeding season, they use these skills to steal from other birds.

When sea birds return from their feeding trips with food for their young, the frigate birds snatch it from them or pester them until they drop it. They will even fly down and, with perfect timing, grab the food just as it is being passed from adult to chick. Frigate birds make their own nests from bones, feathers and twigs broken from trees as they fly past.

▲ Frigate birds have long, narrow pointed wings like all long-distance ocean fliers.

▼ When breeding, the male develops a red throat pouch. He inflates it like a balloon to attract a female.

Outside the breeding season, frigate birds have to catch their own food. They take fish, squid and jellyfish from the surface of the water. They are careful not to go into the water, for their feathers are not waterproof and they cannot swim.

Hornbill

BIRD THAT IMPRISONS ITSELF

With their large bills, hornbills look as if they should be clumsy birds. In fact they are not. The extra piece, the casque, that some of them have on the top of the bill is made of light, spongy bone.

Most hornbills live in the hot, wet rainforests of Africa and Asia. They nest in hollows in trees, often those made by woodpeckers. After the female has laid her eggs, she imprisons herself in the hollow by blocking the entrance with a 'cement' of mud and saliva. Sometimes the male helps her.

▲ A male yellow-billed hornbill feeding his chicks. A section of the tree trunk has been replaced with glass, but the male still feeds the chicks through the usual hole.

The two birds fill the entrance until there is only a narrow slit left. The male then feeds his mate while she sits on the eggs. She may be there for between one and four months. In this closed-off hollow, the female and her eggs, or chicks, are safe from predators.

The female of some kinds of hornbill breaks out of her prison when the chicks have hatched. The chicks repair the entrance themselves and then the adult birds feed them through the slit.

◀ The male hornbill feeds the female while she is imprisoned in the tree. He may bring her over 24,000 fruits during the time that she stays there.

Hummingbird

SHIMMERING NECTAR-EATER

Hummingbirds spend their active hours flitting in search of nectar. Their wings beat so fast, 50–80 times a second, that the wings become a blur and make a humming noise. Some can fly at 113 kph. They can jerk to a stop, hover, and even fly backwards because their wings can swivel in all directions. Flying in this way uses up large amounts of energy, so hummingbirds must feed nearly all the time they are on the move.

Although hummingbirds take nectar from flowers, the flowers get something in return. Each time the bird visits a flower, grains of pollen stick to its body. When it visits another flower, the pollen is passed on. In this way, flowers are fertilized and can produce their seeds.

▲ An Anna's hummingbird feeding. Most hummingbirds have long bills for reaching into the centre of flowers. The nectar is sucked up through the tongue which is long and tubular.

At night, when hummingbirds are not able to feed, they slow down almost completely. They go into a state which is more than just an ordinary form of sleep – it is a kind of night-time hibernation called torpor. Their bodies use very little energy at this time.

▼ A Costa's hummingbird approaching a flower. With their incredibly fast wing-speeds, hummingbirds are able to hover over flowers while they feed.

Kiwi

RUNNING BIRD

The kiwi is the smallest running bird in the southern hemisphere, or southern part of the world, and the national emblem of New Zealand. It is 25–40 cm long, with stout legs, strong claws and a long, slender bill. It has wings, but these are very small and hidden among the hair-like feathers. Like many island-living birds that have never had to escape from fierce predators, the kiwi is flightless.

At night, the kiwi comes out of its burrow, and waddles about in the dimly lit pine forests of its home. When the ground is moist and soft, the bird drives its bill into the soil to pull out worms,

insects and larvae. During the summer, when the ground is hard, it eats fruits and leaves.

The female kiwi lays one or two eggs, which the male incubates, or keeps warm. These are large eggs for the size of the bird, being around 12 per cent of the female's weight. In comparison, an ostrich egg is only about 1 per cent of the bird's weight.

The kiwi's nostrils are at the end of its beak and it appears to find its food by smell. This is unusual, as most birds do not have a good sense of smell.

▼ The kiwi comes out to feed at night. It has weak eyesight, but large ears. If it senses danger, it dashes for cover.

Mallee Fowl

MOUND-BUILDERS

Most birds incubate, or keep their eggs warm, by sitting on them – the heat comes from their bodies. However, the mallee fowl from Australia incubates its eggs another way: it builds an incubator.

At the onset of winter, the male bird digs a pit that is about 60–90 cm deep and about 3 m across. He fills it with wet leaves, twigs and grass, and then covers it with sand. The vegetation begins to rot and gives off heat.

When the male thinks that the temperature is right, he scoops out a hole and the female lays her first egg. Throughout the next six months, she continues to lay eggs at intervals until there are about thirty-three of them in the mound.

The young mallee fowls hatch at intervals, dig their way out of the mound, and are ignored by their parents. They run off and have to look after themselves.

▲ Here the male mallee fowl is testing the temperature of the mound for one last time as the female moves in to lay her egg.

The male mallee fowl adds or removes sand from the mound to keep it at a constant temperature of 33°C while the eggs are incubating. He tests the temperature at regular intervals with his tongue.

▶ The mallee fowl's nest is a mound of rotting plant material and sand. The areas in which they nest are dry, with few plants, and so the male has to gather the leaves and grass from a wide area.

Mockingbird

COPY-CAT SINGER

Singing comes naturally to birds, but few sing such a variety of songs as the mockingbird. There are several species, but the best known is the northern mockingbird of the southern USA.

This mockingbird is 23–25 cm long with a slender bill and tail, and rather drab, grey plumage. What it lacks in looks it makes up for musically. The song is a lovely burbling melody which changes continually. The bird may sing a favourite song many times, and then abandon it and make up a new one.

In each song, there are many notes that are copied from elsewhere, such as human voices or even sounds from machinery. Other birds are sometimes mimicked exactly. When nightingales were taken to Florida for example, the resident mockingbirds copied their song note for note.

Mockingbirds are not everyone's favourite bird – they have a taste for fruit of all kinds. However, they also eat insects that are harmful to crops.

◀ Mockingbirds live in suburbs, thickets and open woodland. They sit on perches and sing to mark their territories.

Mockingbirds sing all year long to mark their territories. They defend them with great energy, even going as far as to attack dogs and people.

Ostrich

LARGEST LIVING BIRD

On the large, flat, open grasslands of Africa, being tall is an advantage for predators can be seen easily as they approach. Like the giraffe, the ostrich is a walking look-out tower. Half of its 2.4 m height is neck. It is not for itself that an adult ostrich is on the look-out, but for its eggs and chicks. Young are in danger from jackals and other predators.

Before they mate, a male and female ostrich perform a courtship ceremony. They feed together, lifting and dropping their heads in time. Then the male displays to the female. He sits down and sways from side to side, showing off his white plumes and twisting his neck into a corkscrew. Several females will lay their eggs in one nest and then a dominant female looks after them.

▲ An adult ostrich can run at 64 kph and can defend itself with the claws on its strong toes. Its long legs and neck are without feathers. This enables it to lose body heat more easily. Over-heating is a problem for large animals that live in hot places.

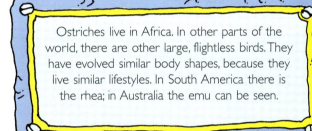

Ostriches live in Africa. In other parts of the world, there are other large, flightless birds. They have evolved similar body shapes, because they live similar lifestyles. In South America there is the rhea; in Australia the emu can be seen.

▼ An ostrich family: the chicks are 30 cm tall when they hatch and can run almost at once. The parents will distract predators from them with displays.

Barn Owl

SOFT-WINGED HUNTER

Barn owls are silent night-time hunters. A barn owl can catch a mouse in total darkness, swooping down on it without being heard. The approach is silent, because the owl's flight feathers are tipped with lighter, fluffier feathers called 'down'. These deaden the noise of the owl's wing beats.

The owl's eyesight is keen, about a hundred times better than ours, but it is their hearing which is most useful to them when hunting.

The owl's ears are set on the side of the bird's head, just behind the eyes. They are in different places on the left and right sides. The sound reaching one ear follows a slightly different path to that going in the other. From the difference between the two, the owl is able to work out exactly where its prey is hiding.

Barn owls swallow their prey whole and later regurgitate (bring up) pellets made of the bones and fur.

▲ Barn owls nest in empty houses, barns and old sheds. The female lays four to seven eggs. The hungry chicks are fed by both parents.

The barn owl holds the record for being the most widely spread land bird in the world. It can be found in every continent except Antarctica. However, they are becoming rare in the British Isles because their preferred roosting places are disappearing.

▼ Barn owls begin their night of hunting as darkness falls. They patrol a regular route, searching for mice, shrews, rats and insects.

Woodpecker

WOOD-BORERS

Woodpeckers are superbly well-adapted to life on the branches and trunks of trees. There are over 200 different species of woodpecker around the world. Most of them eat insects, both adults and young, which they find in crevices, under the bark or in the wood of trees.

A woodpecker searching for insects hops up the trunk of a tree. Backward-pointing claws on its feet help it to grip. It climbs in a spiral path, and chops into the wood with its sharp bill. Once a hole has been made, the bird pushes its long tongue into the hole – some green woodpeckers have tongues that are 15 cm long. Any insects are picked up by barbs or sticky saliva on the end of the tongue.

▲ Inside the nest of a great spotted woodpecker. Here, the chicks are safe from predators and extreme weather.

Woodpeckers use their wood-boring abilities to make a nest. They carve their way into the trunk and then down to make a cavity which may be up to 30 cm deep.

In the deserts of the USA there are woodpeckers who make their nests in the thick trunks of saguaro cacti. In later years these holes become the homes of other desert-living birds, including owls and sparrowhawks.

◄ This adult pileated woodpecker is feeding his young by regurgitating food and putting it directly into his chicks' mouths.

Pelican

FISHING BIRD

Pelicans are among the strangest-looking birds. They look clumsy and ungainly but, in fact, are superb fliers and swimmers. Some of the larger species of pelican have a wingspan of 3 m, and can fly at over 40 kph for long distances. They often fly together, in a V-formation, with their wings beating in time with each other.

Pelicans catch fish by using their bills as if they were nets. A pelican's bill is flat on top, but the bottom part has a pouch which will stretch to hold 9 litres of water. White pelicans feed on the surface, dipping their bills into the water to scoop up fish.

▲ Brown pelicans dive into the water from above. The noise as they hit the water is so loud that it may stun fish swimming just below the surface.

▼ A grey pelican.

Pelicans sometimes fish together. They line up and beat the water with their wings, driving the fish into shallow water where they can be scooped up easily.

Penguin

FROZEN SURVIVORS

At 105 cm tall, emperor penguins are the largest penguins. They live in the seas around Antarctica. The adults come on to land to breed in May. After courtship and mating, each female lays a single egg and then returns to the sea to feed. The male keeps the egg warm by resting it on his feet and covering it with a fold of skin from his belly.

During the six to eight cold weeks which follow, the males do not feed. They become sluggish, keeping warm by huddling together. The females return with stores of squid in a part of their stomach called the crop, just as the eggs are hatching. It is then the males' turn to go and feed. They may have to walk many miles to reach the sea.

▲ With their torpedo-shaped bodies, these king penguins, like all penguins, are well-suited to swimming. They have dense oily feathers and a layer of blubber beneath the skin for keeping out the cold. Their wings are too small for flight, but make very good paddles.

Emperor penguins can stay under water for up to fifteen minutes to depths of 265 m. When a penguin is diving, its heartbeat slows down. The blood flows more slowly around the bird's body and it uses less oxygen.

▼ A colony of emperor penguins may be made up of many thousands of birds. These males are incubating eggs. They are huddling together for warmth in temperatures as low as –50° C.

Peregrine Falcon

BIRD OF SPEED

The peregrine falcon is a bird of prey – it hunts and catches other birds, especially pigeons, and small mammals. It catches them as it flies, with a dive, or stoop, of breathtaking speed and accuracy. Peregrine falcons live on open moors and forests all over the world, but are most common in rocky areas on mountains or along the coasts. Each pair will stay together for life, and use the same nesting site year after year.

For centuries, birds of prey, such as peregrine falcons, have been kept and flown by falconers. They have been trained to catch and return game, such as hares, grouse and bustards. In recent years, they have been kept at airports to scare smaller birds from runways.

▲ Peregrine falcons have been recorded diving through the air at speeds of 355 kph, making them the fastest birds in the world.

In many countries the number of peregrine falcons has fallen. Insecticides from the animals on which the falcon feeds, build up in the bird's body with each animal eaten. The poisons affect the bird's eggs, which become thin and easily broken, or else the chicks die. Recently, some countries have stopped using certain dangerous chemicals and peregrine falcons are on the increase.

▼ Peregrines snatch birds from their perches or catch them in flight. Small mammals are plucked from the ground. The bird then carries its prey to a favourite feeding perch.

Swift

GREATEST FLIERS

Swifts spend nearly all their lives in the air. They eat insects and other small animals that fly or float in the air, scooping them up into their gaping mouths as they fly.

Bad or cold weather means fewer flying insects, so they are found where it is warm. They are able to avoid bad weather by flying away from it, even flying right around storms if necessary. Common swifts breed in northern Europe in the summer, but leave for southern Africa when the winter comes.

Swifts that are ready to breed have to land. They mate in the air, and gather the materials they need for their nests, such as feathers, paper and straw, while flying. Non-breeding swifts fly high into the air at night. They roost on the

▲ The common swift nests in buildings. This one has chosen to build in the wall of a castle. Two to three eggs are laid in the nest.

wing, taking short naps between bouts of flapping.

Swifts, swallows and martins all have long pointed wings. Swallows and martins both have white underparts, but only swallows have long tail-streamers. Swifts are black-brown all over except for a white chin-patch.

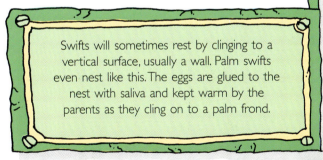

Swifts will sometimes rest by clinging to a vertical surface, usually a wall. Palm swifts even nest like this. The eggs are glued to the nest with saliva and kept warm by the parents as they cling on to a palm frond.

◀ The long, narrow wings of swifts are built for speed. They feed, mate, collect nest material and sometimes sleep on the wing. They drink by dipping their bills into the water as they fly over it, and bathe by splashing into it and quickly taking off again.

Arctic Tern

LONG-DISTANCE FLIER

These lightly built sea birds look as if they would be blown away by a strong wind, and yet they are able to fly incredible distances.

Arctic terns breed inside the Arctic circle during the northern summer. They feed on small fish and crustaceans – animals with hard outer skin, such as shrimps – which they pluck from the sea by skimming low over the waves.

When the winter comes, the coastal waters freeze and the terns set off on a long migration. They fly south, over the equator and halfway around the world, to the pack-ice of the Antarctic, and enjoy the southern summer. They stay there until winter comes and then fly north to the Arctic again.

This is a round trip of about 38,625 km, but by commuting in this way, the terns enjoy two summers, or one long one lasting about eight months.

▲ There are several species of terns. They all have long wings and plumage in different combinations of white, grey and black.

There are many birds that migrate long distances. It is thought that they find their way by using the Sun during the day and the stars at night. Scientists believe they are also sensitive to the Earth's magnetic field, so that they know which way is south and which is north.

▼ Terns are easy to tell from gulls because they have pointed wings and forked tails. They have a slow, bouncing flight like that of a butterfly, holding their heads as if they are looking down.

Weaver Bird

AMAZING NEST BUILDERS

Weaver birds are sparrow-sized birds from Africa and Asia. There are seventy different kinds. Most of them eat seeds, especially grass seeds, but some eat insects, running up and down tree trunks to find them in the bark. For part of the year, both males and females are a dull brown colour, but in the breeding season the males have bright plumage. They live wherever there are trees in which to make their nests.

The males are the nest builders. The first strands of grass or strips of palm leaf are woven into a loop. This is added to until it becomes a hollow ball. Attached to this is an entrance which may be 60 cm long.

When the woven nest is complete, the male displays at the entrance, showing off his yellow or red plumage, hoping to attract a female. If he succeeds, his mate will then line the nest with soft grass tops and lay her eggs.

▲ A golden weaver bird from Malawi building his nest among the reeds.

▼ A male spotted back weaver bird displays for a female at the entrance to his neatly built nest.

In some kinds of weaver bird, the males make several nests and attract a female for each one. Even after there are no more available females, they carry on building nests, which will be left empty or unfinished.

Anteater

LONGEST TONGUE OF ALL

When they are not sleeping, which they do for fourteen to fifteen hours a day, giant anteaters shuffle between ants' nests looking for food. They are very well-equipped for eating their tiny prey.

On their front feet anteaters have sharp, powerful claws which are 4–10 cm long. They use these to open up, but not demolish, the ants' nest. Then they thrust their long noses inside the nest and lap up the ants with their tongues.

An anteater's tongue can be pushed out an incredible 60 cm, at a rate of 150 times a minute. It is covered with tiny spines and coated in large amounts of sticky saliva – ants stick to it helplessly. An anteater will take only about 140 ants from one nest before moving on to

▲ All anteaters have an extremely good sense of smell. They sniff out ants' nests and break them open with their strong claws. They are careful not to destroy the nest completely. This is a giant anteater.

another. By grazing in this way, it makes sure that the nests in its home territory will survive to be feasted upon another day.

Anteaters protect their long claws by walking on their knuckles. This makes them look as if they are limping.

◀ An adult tamandua, or lesser anteater, and her darker baby eating ants. The tamandua is a tree-dwelling anteater. It has long claws and a tail which can wrap itself around branches.

Armadillo

ARMOURED MAMMAL

With its suit of hard, bony plates, the armadillo is the most heavily armoured animal living today. It has shields over its shoulders, hips, tail, head and parts of its legs. When frightened, the armadillo pulls its legs up under its body and sits tight. There are twenty different species, living in deserts, grasslands and forests of Central and South America.

The common long-nosed armadillo is the most widespread. It uses its keen sense of smell to find small animals and insects, and then digs them out of the ground. It digs with its front claws and kicks the soil behind it with its back legs. This armadillo will eat roots, fungi and fruits, but mostly it prefers ants and termites – up to 40,000 in one meal.

▲ The different species of armadillo can be told apart by the number of plates or bands that cover their bodies. This is an eleven-banded armadillo.

The armadillo's young are born in the spring when there is plenty of food to eat. Common long-nosed armadillos have four babies of the same sex, that is, they are all either male or female.

▼ A six-banded armadillo from eastern South America.

Bat

HUNTING BY SOUND

There are over 900 different kinds of bat and they are found all over the world. Although they have wings and so look rather like birds, they do not have feathers or lay eggs. They are mammals: the females give birth to live young and feed them on milk.

Some bats are expert fliers, and are able to turn in tight spaces with great agility. They are the only mammals that can fly by flapping their wings – others, such as the flying squirrel, use their 'wings' of skin to glide through the air.

Bats find their way about at night, and catch their food, with sound. They make very high-pitched sounds, which humans cannot hear. When these sounds hit an object, they return as echoes. From these, bats can tell whether the object is moving or standing still and how far away it is.

▲ The long-eared bat catches insects in flight and can also pick them off leaves. Its large ears enable it to pick up returning echoes.

▼ Mexican free-tailed bats flying at sunset.

Bats eat all sorts of food, including fruit, fish, pollen and even blood. A large number of them eat insects, which they catch at night while flying. Each bat recognizes the sound of its own voice. This means that even if hunting with others, it cannot be distracted by the sounds they make.

Beaver

DAM BUILDERS

Beavers are the great builders of the animal world, and are able to change the places in which they live.

The first thing a beaver does when it moves to a new river is to build a dam. It fells saplings, or young trees, by gnawing through their trunks with its powerful teeth. Then it hauls them into position. With its agile front paws, it then builds in-between the branches with mud, stones and smaller sticks.

The dam blocks the flow of the water and a pond is formed. In the middle of this pond, the beaver builds its lodge. The lodge is hollowed out. There inside, the young are born, safe from enemies.

▲ Lodges are sometimes passed on from one generation to another. It is thought that some have been occupied for a thousand years.

▼ Beavers are slow and clumsy on land, but with their torpedo-shaped bodies and webbed feet, they are good swimmers. They move along by flapping their flattened tails up and down.

The beavers' young, or kits, are born within the safety of the lodge. They can swim within days but cannot dive along the lodge's underwater passages to the pond, because they float too easily.

Hippopotamus

WATER-LOVING GIANTS

The hippopotamus is second in size only to the elephant, and is up to 4 m long. Just like all large animals, one of its main problems is keeping cool. Hippos solve this by spending the hot African days in water. At night, when it is cooler, they come out of the water to feed on grass.

Females and their young live together in a group, often in the middle of a river on a raised bank. Several males live alone around the edge of the group, and are not allowed to come near without permission from the females.

The babies are about 90 cm long at birth. The mother takes her youngster on to the land and teaches it to stay close to her. She butts it with her head if it disobeys and licks it when it does the right thing. In the animal world, deliberate teaching like this is rare.

▲ This male is not yawning, but showing his tusks to other males as a warning. Male hippos fight for the right to live close to the females, often gashing each other badly with their 30–60 cm tusks.

The hippo's eyes, ears and nostrils are on the top of its head. This enables it to stand or sit almost completely covered by water with as little as possible showing above the surface. The hippo's skin is protected by a pink oily substance. This is known as 'pink sweat'.

Flying Lemur

LIVING KITE

The flying lemur was not well named, because it is not really a lemur and it does not fly, it glides. Another name for this animal, which is classified in a family of its own, is the colugo.

It has a membrane of skin from its neck to the tip of its tail, taking in the front arms and fingers and the back legs and toes. When these limbs are stretched out, the flying lemur looks like a kite.

The flying lemur lives in rainforests and spends most of its time in the trees. Many of these trees are very tall and it is up in the branches that it finds most of its food. If the animal went down to the ground when it wanted to move from

▲ A flying lemur, or colugo, with her baby. She is safe from predators in the trees and will rarely venture to the ground. She moves from tree to tree by gliding.

Lemurs are nocturnal animals – they rest during the day and feed on leaves, buds and flowers at night. Their large eyes give them good night-time vision.

one tree to another, it might be caught by a predator. So the flying lemur glides between the trees. It runs up the trees and launches itself from the top. It can glide as far as 70 m and, over that distance, will only lose about 12 m in height.

◀ A baby flying lemur clings to its mother's fur and feeds on her milk. It goes with her everywhere, even when she glides.

Meerkat

SUN-WORSHIPPERS

Meerkats are a kind of mongoose and live in colonies of up to twenty-four individuals. They are burrowers, making their homes in the dry, open grasslands of southern Africa. Meerkats spend the day above ground, often just basking in the sunshine. While some groom each other or feed, others watch for danger. If a hawk or eagle flies by, a look-out will bark and the colony watches it closely until it has gone.

Meerkats do not travel far from their burrows and soon eat all the food in the area. When this happens, they just move on and dig new burrows elsewhere. Meerkats eat almost anything, including insects, roots, lizards, rats and birds. They can attack poisonous snakes as they seem to be immune to their venom.

▲ Meerkats keep watch by standing up on their back legs and balancing with their tails.

An enemy on the ground may be approached by a growling meerkat with its legs outstretched and back arched. Sometimes, a group of meerkats will advance together. This may look to the intruder as if a larger animal is coming towards it.

▼ An adult female meerkat acting as babysitter. The young ones at her feet are the offspring of others.

Jumping Mouse

LITTLE HIGH JUMPERS

Jumping mice are made to jump. They have long back feet, strong back legs and long tails to help them balance when in mid-air. It is disappointing then to learn that the most common kinds move about under vegetation in a series of short hops. The woodland jumping mouse, however, does live up to its name; it gets about in leaps that are 1.5–3 m long.

Jumping mice live in North America and in the northern parts of Europe and Asia. When it gets cold in the winter, they find a burrow in which to hide and make a nest. Then they hibernate. Many animals hibernate throughout the cold, dark winters. They go into a deep sleep. Their body temperature falls and their

▲ A jumping mouse reaching up for some fruit. With their strong back legs these mice can jump 1.5–3 m in a single leap.

Badgers, woodchuck, hedgehogs, dormice and ground squirrels are all examples of hibernating animals. They live in places where the winters are long, cold and dark. Going into a deep sleep somewhere safe and warm is a way of surviving these harsh conditions.

heartbeat and breathing slow down. During this long sleep they live on fat they have stored in their bodies. Jumping mice hibernate for six to nine months of the year, but wake every two weeks, probably to urinate. During its sleep, the body temperature of a hibernating mouse falls to just above freezing point (0°C).

◄ This grasshopper mouse is howling a challenge to other males during the mating season.

Mole

DIGGER IN THE DARK

Moles are very well adapted for digging, and it is an activity which keeps them busy day and night. Their eyes are small, for they are of little use in the dark, but their senses of smell and hearing are good. Moles are also very sensitive to vibrations, and can 'feel' a predator walking over the ground or the wriggling of a worm nearby.

Moles can move quickly just under the surface of the ground, heaving the soil up in a ridge. They also dig a system of tunnels which are constantly repaired and extended. Soil is heaved outside to form molehills. Oval nesting chambers are made and lined with grass and leaves. The 3–4 babies are blind and naked at birth, but soon grow fur and can see.

▲ The star-nosed mole, from North America, has 22 small, fleshy 'tentacles' on the end of its snout. It uses these to feel for its food, which is mainly insect larvae, shrimps and small fish caught in water, and earthworms from the soil.

▼ An eastern mole from the east of North America. Its broad front feet are used for digging tunnels.

With their powerful front feet, moles tunnel through the soil in an action which is very like swimming the breast-stroke. Digging is hungry work and moles need to eat regularly. During times of plenty, they will store worms in special places to eat later.

Porcupine

PRICKLY DEFENDER

There are porcupines in the New World (North and South America) and in the Old World (Asia, Africa and Europe). The two groups are quite different, the main difference being that New World porcupines are tree-climbers, while those in the rest of the world live entirely on the ground.

The North American porcupine is about 1 m long and clumsily built, but a good climber just the same. The animal's long hair hides its secret weapons: 20,000 spines with sharp tips. When the animal is threatened, these are raised and rattled as a warning to the predator to keep away.

▲ An African porcupine. Its quills are standing up in a threatening posture, perhaps because it is alarmed by the presence of the photographer.

Porcupines are said to be extremely fond of salt. They will gnaw the handles of tools which have been gripped by sweaty palms and even eat broken glass in an attempt to get at the salt that it contains.

If the threat continues, the porcupine will run backwards at its enemy. The spines are only loosely embedded in the porcupine's skin and come out easily. Once in the face or skin of an attacker, they can be difficult to remove and can work their way deep into the animal's flesh. The wounds may then become infected, causing a great deal of pain and even death. Baby porcupines are born with their spines, but at that time the spines are soft. They take about ten days to harden.

◀ A tree porcupine, or coendou, from South America. This species has a prehensile tail which it can wrap around branches, making it a good climber.

Skunk

TWO-TONE STINKER

The skunk's distinctive black-and-white colouring is a warning to a predator that it should not attack. If an enemy comes too close, the skunk will lower its head, raise its tail and stamp its front paws. If this warning is ignored, the skunk will spin around and spray over its attacker a foul-smelling liquid from glands near its tail.

Skunks rarely miss their target if it is within 3.5 m. This liquid can cause blindness for a short time and its strong smell can be detected over half a mile away. Understandably, most predators,

▲ A spotted skunk on the prowl. When startled or attacked, they turn themselves up into a 'hand-stand' position and spray.

Unfortunately, many skunks are killed by cars. They have not yet learnt that traffic is dangerous. When faced with an on-coming car, they tend to stand their ground and raise their tail in the hope that the car will be warned away.

such as bobcats and pumas, keep away from skunks unless they are very hungry.

Striped skunks range from southern Canada, throughout the USA to northern Mexico. They are about 75 cm long with a 30-cm tail and can be found in woods, grasslands and desert areas. They sleep in a burrow during the day and come out to feed at night on insects, frogs, birds and eggs.

◀ A striped skunk. This species launches its foul-smelling weapon by turning its back on its enemy and lifting its tail.

Brown Bear

NORTHERN WANDERER

Brown bears wander continuously over their range looking for food. Their diet changes throughout the year, depending on what is most available. In spring, they eat eggs and the young of lemmings and ground squirrels. In autumn, fruits and berries are a favourite food, but roots and leaves are eaten all year round.

Bears that live in the cold forests of the north sleep in dens in the winter. This is not hibernation, just a deep sleep. Here the cubs are born – they are tiny and without fur. The mother feeds them with her milk while she lives on the fat she has stored in her body during the autumn. The family emerges some time between April and June.

▲ Bears can stand up on their hind legs to get a better view of their surroundings.

▼ Brown bears usually live alone, but at certain times of the year several can be seen catching salmon from the same stretch of river.

Brown bears are found in Alaska and North America, northern Europe and Asia. The largest in America are the Kodiak bears of the far north-west. They can weigh up to 442 kg and can stand 3 m tall on their back legs.

Polar Bear

WHITE BEAR OF THE FROZEN NORTH

Polar bears live on the southern edge of the Arctic pack-ice. This is close to the sea, where pieces of ice break off, and where seals come to breed and rest. The bears feed on the seals, particularly ringed seals. They lie in wait beside the seals' breathing holes, or creep up on the seals as they rest on the surface of the ice.

The bears will travel long distances, up to 70 km, each day in search of food. In the winter, they travel south as the sea freezes and the ice-pack becomes larger. In the summer, they make their way north again.

At the beginning of winter, the female will stop roaming and make a den in the snow, where she gives birth to two or three cubs. The mother's milk is high in fat, and on this rich diet her cubs grow quickly and are able to stay warm. They emerge from their snowy home in March or April and stay with their mother for another two years.

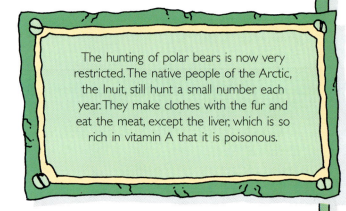

The hunting of polar bears is now very restricted. The native people of the Arctic, the Inuit, still hunt a small number each year. They make clothes with the fur and eat the meat, except the liver, which is so rich in vitamin A that it is poisonous.

▼ Polar bears are well suited to their life in the cold. Their white fur camouflages them against the snow, and it is thick and waterproof. A layer of fat beneath the skin keeps it warm. Except for the nose and small pads on the soles of the feet, every part of a bear's body is covered with fur. The furry soles help the animal to grip the ice when walking.

Cheetah

FASTEST ANIMAL ON LAND

Cheetahs hunt the small antelopes of the African grasslands, such as gazelles and impalas. They have two methods of hunting. In the first, they stroll up to a group of grazing animals, looking disinterested but actually choosing one which is slightly apart from the rest.

The second method entails them creeping up on the victim slowly, with their bodies pressed low to the ground. Then, when they are close enough, the cheetahs give chase with a burst of energy. They can reach 72 kph in just two seconds and have a top speed of 113 kph. The victim is knocked to the ground and killed by a suffocating bite to the throat.

Cheetahs are built for speed, not stamina, and so can only run fast over short distances. If the antelope gets a head start, a cheetah will soon abandon the chase. In one chase in two, adult gazelles get away.

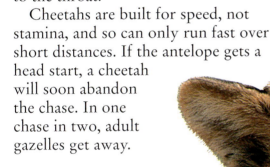

▲ Gazelles are fast runners, but the cheetah is faster, at least over short distances. The cheetah's backbone bends, or flexes, as it sprints, giving it extra speed. Cheetahs have the longest legs of all the big cats – although they have the same sized body as a leopard, at over 90 cm, they stand 30 cm taller than a leopard.

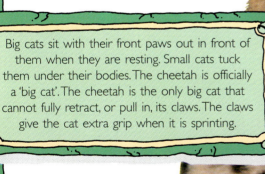

Big cats sit with their front paws out in front of them when they are resting. Small cats tuck them under their bodies. The cheetah is officially a 'big cat'. The cheetah is the only big cat that cannot fully retract, or pull in, its claws. The claws give the cat extra grip when it is sprinting.

Hunting Dog

SOCIAL KILLERS

Hunting dogs are fierce meat-eaters that live on the grasslands of Africa. They rest, hunt, travel and breed in groups, but the way those groups are organized is most unusual.

In most other mammals that live together in groups, such as lions, the females are related and form a group which wandering males may join. In hunting dogs, it is the other way around. In any one group of up to thirty dogs, all the adult males will be brothers, and all the adult females will be from another pack. Unless there are young pups, the group moves continuously across its home range, looking for food. The adults share the kill, but usually let the pups feed first.

▲ A pack of African hunting dogs about to kill a wildebeeste. These dogs hunt in a co-operative way, spreading out and then closing in on the victim in such a way that it cannot escape.

In each group of hunting dogs, only one male and female pair will breed at a time. This pair also leads the hunt.

▼ Hunting dogs have a greeting ceremony; they run around excitedly, squeaking and nuzzling each other. Males also have harmless play fights.

Fennec Fox

BIG-EARED DESERT DWELLER

This quick-witted animal is the smallest of all the foxes, and the one with the biggest ears. It lives in the deserts of North Africa where it is scorching hot in the day and very cold at night. The fennec fox avoids the worst of the heat by staying underground in its burrow during the day. This burrow can be up to 10.5 m long, and is dug into the side of a hill or mound.

The fennec fox's large ears have two uses: they have a large surface area and so they help it to lose body heat. They are also very good at picking up sounds. At night, the fennec fox listens for sounds made by the animals it eats, such as gerbils, birds, snakes and scorpions, and those made by animals that wish to eat it, like hyenas and jackals.

▲ The fennec fox's ears help it to keep cool during the day; its fur keeps it warm at night.

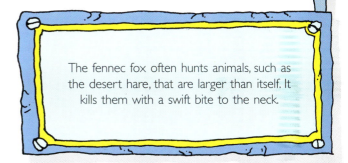

The fennec fox often hunts animals, such as the desert hare, that are larger than itself. It kills them with a swift bite to the neck.

Mongoose

SNAKE-KILLER

Mongooses are alert and active mammals with sleek bodies and sharp teeth. They are famous for their ability to kill poisonous snakes, but they will eat almost any small animals, including insects, lizards, birds, mice and rats.

Eggs are one of their chief delights and they have two ways of cracking them open. One is to grip the egg with the front paws and roll it under their body, through the back legs, and against a rock. The other is to rear up holding the egg and come down with it hard against the ground.

Snake killing requires lightning-fast movements and lots of courage. The mongoose has both and also has some immunity to the snake's venom.

▲ A 1-m long mongoose can overcome a cobra nearly twice its size. If the snake strikes, the mongoose will dodge smartly out of the way. It eventually kills the snake by biting its neck.

In the past, mongooses have been taken to many islands in the hope that they would control the number of snakes. Unfortunately, they also attack birds and small mammals, and have brought many to the brink of extinction.

▼ A pair of yellow mongooses.

Stoat

FAST-CHANGE ARTIST

Stoats have long bodies and short legs. When they run, they seem to ripple along the ground. They are fast and agile hunters, and will pursue their prey into holes, along tunnels, up trees and into water. They are total meat eaters, or carnivores, eating rabbits, hares, moles, mice, rats and birds.

Stoats are found in Europe, Asia and North America. In northern areas where it snows, stoats go through a complete colour change. Usually, they are red-brown with yellowy underparts: perfect camouflage for the woods and hedges where they hunt. In the winter, a new coat of white hair grows underneath the old one. In the spring, the white coat is moulted back to the familiar red-brown.

▲ In both its red-brown and white coat, the stoat has a distinctive black tip to its tail.

▼ A stoat in its (ermine) winter coat. In this phase it is well-camouflaged against the snows of winter.

The red-brown coat can be moulted in just three days, so that the animal seems to turn white almost overnight. A stoat in its white winter coat is known as an ermine. In Britain, the ceremonial robes of nobility and royalty have always been trimmed with ermine.

Tiger

STRIPED HUNTERS

Tigers have always filled humans with fear and fascination, and with good reason, for they are perfectly made killers. Tigers usually hunt animals such as deer and wild pigs, and they are very well coloured for stalking and ambushing their prey.

The tiger's stripes break up its outline, making it hard to see, especially in long grass. The tiger stays low, in a crouch position with its head up, until it is within about 20 m of its prey. Then it leaps out, covers the remaining distance in a few bounds, and brings the animal to the ground. In spite of their efforts, tigers do not easily catch their prey. Nine out of ten animals get away unhurt.

▲ The biggest tigers reach over 3 m in length, and this makes them the largest of the big cats. They have long back legs, strong front legs, and paws armed with long, sharp claws.

Tigers once lived all across Asia, but there are now fewer than ever. Their forest home is being turned into farmland, and they are hunted for their bones, claws and skins. Buying and selling tiger parts is illegal in many countries, but not all. In some countries, especially India, there are reserves in which tigers are protected.

▼ Tigers are the only big cats who like bathing – the water helps them to stay cool. They often reverse slowly into the water because they do not like to get their faces wet.

Bison

GIANT OF THE PLAINS

The sight of two adult bull (male) bisons fighting is a spectacular one. They usually only fight in the breeding season, when each bull is trying to win the right to mate with the females. Fights begin with displays of bellowing, rolling in the dust and head swaying. Usually, one will back down, but if it does not, the two will fight.

They slam their heads together making lumps of hair fly in the air. They circle each other, turning quickly and lunging with their horns in an attempt to injure their opponent.

About sixty million bison once roamed the Great Plains – the vast open grassland of North America. They moved continually in search of fresh grass. In the nineteenth century, they were hunted almost to extinction by white hunters who killed them for their hides, but some were saved and protected in nature reserves, such as Yellowstone National Park.

▼ The bison's humped shoulders are covered in long shaggy hair. The soft, woolly hair of the hindparts and lower parts is moulted in the spring. Bison may be from 3 to 4 m long.

When the great herds of bison, or buffalo as they are also known, roamed the Great Plains, they migrated, or travelled, south in the winter and north in the summer. They followed traditional routes known as the buffalo trails.

Camel

ULTIMATE DESERT-DWELLER

Camels are very well suited, or adapted, to lands that are hot during the day, cold at night, and lacking in water and lush vegetation, such as the Sahara Desert in Africa or the Gobi Desert in central Asia.

Camels eat a wide variety of plants, including thorns and salt bushes, which other animals will not touch. They are able to travel long distances in search of food because they have an amazing ability to go without water for long periods. Camels store water in their body tissues, and an animal that is not working can go ten months without drinking. By that time it will be thin and unhealthy. If it finds water it can drink 135 litres in ten minutes, its body swelling and returning to normal as it drinks.

There are two types of camel: dromedaries (mostly found in Africa and Arabia) have one hump, while bactrians (from the Gobi Desert) have two humps. The humps are stores of energy-rich fat. This fat can be used to give the animals energy if they have to go without food.

▲ Camels have long eye-lashes to keep wind-blown sand out of their eyes. The fur is thick: this keeps the animal warm at night and insulates it from the heat during the day.

For thousands of years camels have been crucial to the lives of the people who live in the deserts of Africa and Asia. Not only do they carry people and goods, but they are also presented as gifts at marriages and paid as fines for injury or murder. Camels were also imported into Australia, where some escaped and established wild herds in the central deserts.

◀ Desert people use dromedaries for riding on. Bactrians, shown here, are stronger and more suitable for carrying loads.

Elephant

LARGEST LAND ANIMAL

With their ears flapping and trunks waving, African elephants travel long distances every day in search of food and water. Some live in open grasslands, others in dense forest. Female, or cow, elephants live together in herds, which are led by one older female. Males, or bulls, usually live alone. The largest male may be 3 m high and weigh 3,000 kg.

An elephant's trunk is a long, muscular upper lip. It is strong and can lift whole trees, but is also very sensitive to smell and touch. At the tip are finger-like lips that can pick up very small objects. The large ears help the elephant to stay cool. The ears have a large number of blood vessels, and as blood travels round them, heat is lost to the air.

▼ Elephants drink by sucking water up into their trunks and squirting it out into their mouths. Like most large animals found in hot countries, elephants find it hard to lose body heat. They like to stay cool by spraying water on to their bodies.

▲ Elephants' tusks are actually long teeth. In old bulls they may be 3.5 m in length and weigh 130 kg. The animals use them to prise bark off trees, dig up roots and pull down branches.

There are two kinds of elephants, the African and the smaller Asian. Both are in danger of extinction, mainly because they are hunted and killed for their tusks – these are the source of ivory, used to make ornaments. In many countries, elephants are protected, but ivory is so valuable that poachers still shoot them.

Giraffe

WORLD'S TALLEST ANIMAL

In the wide open grasslands and semi-desert areas of Africa, it helps to be able to see long distances. That way predators can be seen easily and the animals can escape in good time. At around 5.5 m tall, giraffes are like walking watch-towers. Incidentally, giraffes have the same number of neck bones (seven) as every other mammal. Their neck bones are simply longer.

Pairs of male giraffes take part in fights to establish who is the most dominant. They stand side by side and bash each other with their heads. They also twine their necks together. Neither giraffe is badly hurt during the fights.

Male and female giraffes feed in different ways. The males stretch up to feed on the highest branches, while the females lean over to eat the leaves of shorter shrubs. A giraffe's lips are extremely mobile and its tongue can extend an incredible 46 cm.

▲ Adult giraffes can defend themselves with their large and heavy hooves – a kick from them can kill a lion. The young are more in danger, though even they are about 2 m tall at birth.

▼ Giraffes drinking at a waterhole.

Ibex

MOUNTAIN JUMPERS

Ibexes are goat antelopes. They live on mountains at heights of 500 to 5,200 m above sea level. In the summer, ibexes stay high in the mountains feeding on grass and lichen. They may move lower during the winter to avoid deep snow.

Ibexes are very sure-footed animals, able to leap from rock to rock at some speed with perfect balance. To escape an enemy, they run over land that the pursuer would find difficult. If cornered, the ibexes will turn and fight with their horns. There are several races, or types, of ibexes. They live in different parts of Europe, Asia and north-eastern Africa. They can be told apart by the shape of their horns.

▲ Ibexes are sure-footed animals, able to walk and run at high speeds over rocky terrain.

The males fight in the rut, between autumn and December, before the breeding season. Two males face each other, rear up on their back legs and smash their heads together. They are not hurt as the bases of their horns are thick. The winner wins the right to breed with the females.

◀ A male Nubian ibex. Male ibexes fight each other for the right to breed with females. The winners are usually the older animals with the thickest horns, that is, those who are at least six years old.

Moose

WADING GRAZER

At nearly 2.5 m tall and around 820 kg in weight, the moose is the largest living deer. It roams about the wooded areas of Alaska and Canada, especially where there are lakes and rivers. The moose is also found in Europe, in Scandinavia, northern Russia and northern China. There it is known as the elk.

In summer, moose wade into water to eat water-lilies and other water plants, often submerging to reach the roots and stems. In winter, they eat the shoots, leaves and branches of young trees. In harsh winters, moose have a hard time finding enough food – they need to eat a total of 4–5 tonnes of food during the winter months – and may resort to eating bark.

▲ Young moose, or calves, can run with their mothers after ten days and will stay with them for two years. Mothers defend their young from wolves or bears by lashing out with their dangerous hooves.

▼ A male moose with fully grown antlers.

The male moose grows new antlers every year. By August, they are fully grown and are used in fights with other males over the females. The males call for mates with a bellow that echoes through the woods. If they hear an answer, they crash through the brushwood to find the female.

Musk-ox

SNOW-BOUND SURVIVORS

Musk-ox live in the vast, treeless tundra of Canada and Greenland. Here the soil is frozen for most of the year. It is as far north as you can be without going on to the ice-pack of the Arctic.

In the summer, the ground thaws a little and plants, such as grasses and sedges, provide food. At this time, they build up a store of fat on their bodies to help them survive the harsh winters.

The females have only one calf every other year. The young musk-ox has a thick woolly coat and can walk within an hour of being born. Large male musk-oxen stand about 1.5 m high at the shoulders and are about 2.5 m long. Females are smaller.

▼ When they feel threatened, a herd of musk-ox will form a circle and face the enemy. The young hide in the middle. If the enemy, which may be a wolf, walks around the herd, the oxen will wheel round so that the strongest male is facing it.

▲ Before breeding takes place, the males fight for the right to lead the herds. During this time they give off a strong musky smell from glands on their faces. They bang their heads together in ferocious battles which go on until one gives up and wanders off.

In the tundra, winter temperatures can be as low as −70°C, and storms can last for days. In the worst weather, the animals huddle together in herds of up to a hundred. The young ones are placed in the middle and the adults turn their backs to the wind until the worst of the storm has passed.

Giant Panda

BAMBOO DEPENDENT

Giant Pandas are members of the bear family and are found only in south-western China, living in the bamboo forests there. There are only 1,200–1,500 giant pandas left in the wild despite enormous efforts to preserve them. Another species is known as the red or lesser panda – they are related to the raccoons.

Giant pandas are vegetarians and mostly eat just a few species of bamboo. This causes problems when the time comes for that species of bamboo to flower and die because there is then no food for the pandas and quite often they starve.

Giant pandas are solitary animals and spend much of their time eating. They have developed a special extra thumb on each front paw to help them grasp the canes and strip off the leaves. They do not breed often, being solitary, which is another reason why they are declining.

▼ Although giant pandas are officially protected by Chinese law, poachers are still killing them because their pelts (skins) can be sold for large sums of money.

The bamboo family contains various types of grass – the tallest and toughest grass in the world! They grow in dense thickets up to 30 m tall. Bamboo plants can grow at an amazing rate – a metre every two days is not unusual. Bamboo spreads by sending out underground runners. It only flowers at the end of its life when it sets seed and then dies.

Rhino

SINGLE-HORNED HEAVYWEIGHTS

Rhinos live alone and are active mainly in the morning and evening. Most days they walk to water holes to drink, or to find mud baths in which to wallow. Wallowing helps them to stay cool and keeps their skin free of insects. Rhinos have a routine, following the same paths at the same time.

Each rhino has a home range which may overlap with those of others. A communal dung pile is often found where the home ranges overlap. Here, each rhino adds his or her own dung to a pile which may eventually be 1.2 m high and 6 m across.

There are two kinds of rhino in Africa: the white and the black. Both are in danger of becoming extinct. White rhinos are not really white. The name comes from an Afrikaans word *weit* which means 'wide' and refers to the rhino's wide mouth.

▶ White rhinos have a wide, square-shaped mouth with which they graze grass. They grow up to 4 m long and over 1.8 m tall at the shoulder.

▼ Black rhinos have a pointed upper lip which they can curl around twigs and leaves on bushes. They are slightly smaller – about 3.9 m long and 1.8 m tall.

Rhinos are hunted for their horns, which are made into dagger handles and medicine. This hunting has brought all five species of rhino to the brink of extinction. In many places, they are now protected by law and trading in rhino horn is banned, but their horns are valuable and the hunting goes on.

Sloth

HANGING UPSIDE DOWN

Sloths spend almost the whole of their lives hanging upside down in trees, and moving along in slow motion. They live in the rainforests of Central and South America, and are very well-suited to life in the trees.

Sloths hang from branches or vines with the help of hook-like claws, and with their long arms they pull themselves through the trees in search of the leaves and fruit they like to eat. If a sloth is forced to move on the ground, it drags itself along with great difficulty.

The sloths' hair grows the opposite way to most mammals. It grows from the stomach towards the back. This is because the animal is nearly always upside down. With the fur growing this way, the rain is able to run off it easily.

▲ A two-toed sloth. Sloths have one baby at a time, which is born in the trees and clings to its mother's fur as she moves around. The baby feeds on its mother's milk for six to nine months and then begins to eat leaves.

A sloth's fur is made up of a short underfur for warmth, and longer, coarser, outer hairs for extra protection. Tiny green plants grow in grooves on the hair, giving the animals a green tinge. This makes them hard to see among the leaves.

The native peoples of the rainforest hunt sloths for their meat, but the animals are affected much more when their forest home is cut down for timber or to make space for roads, farms, factories or housing.

◄ There are two kinds of sloth: three-toed sloths, pictured here, are 45–60 cm long, and have a short stumpy tail. Two-toed sloths (above) are longer and have no tail.

Springbok

LEAPING GAZELLES

Springboks are a kind of gazelle. They live in south-west Africa and are remarkable for their 'pronking'. These animals live in large herds, and when an enemy, such as a cheetah or a lion, is spotted, one or several members of the herd will give the alarm.

They do this by leaping straight up into the air, as high as 3.5 m, with their legs held stiffly down and their body curved. This is pronking, and each

▲ Pronking tells other members of the herd that there is danger near, it enables the animal to see further and it may also help to confuse the enemy.

In the past, huge numbers of springbok would build up in an area, and then suddenly migrate because of the shortage of food. Herds of up to a million animals would sweep across the land in a tide, picking up other kinds of gazelles as well that got in the way. In recent times, such large numbers have not occurred, because the animals have been hunted so heavily.

animal may pronk several times, making it look as if it is bouncing.

Springboks use also another warning signal. From the middle of the animal's back to its rump is a fold of skin which can suddenly reveal a broad flash of pure white hair. This signal may be given first by one springbok, and then another, so that the white flashing seems to sweep over the herd. Once the enemy has been located, the whole herd will run swiftly away.

Vicuña

MOUNTAIN ANIMALS

Vicuñas are humpless camels from South America. In the same family are the llamas and alpacas, which were once kept by the Incas for their wool and meat, and as animals for carrying heavy loads. Vicuñas, however, are not easy to tame. They live on the Andes mountain ranges at heights ranging from 3,650 to 4,800 m. At these heights it is cold, the winds are fierce and there is less oxygen than at lower altitudes.

Vicuñas are able to survive these conditions because they have a thick woolly coat and because their blood is

▲ Vicuñas live in all-male or family herds. They walk between sleeping and feeding areas with their necks craned forward and can run swiftly from predators.

Every year, herds of vicuñas are rounded up and sheared. Their wool is said to be the finest and lightest of any animal. Thirty years ago they were close to extinction. Today, they are fully protected and their numbers are rising.

different from that of other animals – it has more oxygen-carrying red blood cells. Because of this they are able to make better use of the oxygen that is available. By day, these animals graze the mountain grasslands. At night, they walk higher up to sleep.

◀ Vicuñas are related to llamas and alpacas, all of which are only found in South America. Llamas are the biggest and vicuñas the smallest.

Wildebeest

THE GREAT WANDERERS

These cow-like antelopes live on the grasslands of South and East Africa. During the wet season (in March, April and May), when there is plenty of rain and the plains are green with young grass shoots, the wildebeest are scattered over a wide area. But in the dry season (July, August and September), they go off in search of fresh grass. They gather into huge herds of up to 10,000, walking 48 km every day in their search for food.

Wildebeest eat only the young shoots of grass, while zebra eat the same grass at a later stage of growth. Another grazing animal, the topi, eats the same grass, but when it is old. In this way these animals can all live together in the same area without competing for food.

▲ Blue wildebeest crossing a river. This species is also known as the brindled gnu. They still live in large numbers in the wild.

▼ On the Serengeti Plain in East Africa, these wildebeest are moving west in the dry season. They are going to the river lands to eat the new grass.

Mating takes place during the trek. Every time the huge herd stops, the males run around with their heads held high and herd together groups of females. They defend these females against rival males. These groups only last a few days. When the great herd moves on once again, they break up. The calves are born in the wet season, when there is plenty of food.

Zebra

STRIPED GRAZER

Zebras are instantly recognizable by their stripes, but why do they have them? Some people think that the stripes make it harder for a predator to see them. Others think that the stripes help zebras to recognize each other.

Zebras live in large herds made up of family units. In each family there are several females with their young and one leading male. If he is killed, the family stays together and will in time be led by another male. There are also herds of males who will at times try to kidnap females to start their own family groups.

Lions are the greatest danger to a herd of zebra. Zebras will often mix with other animals, including ostriches. The birds have good eyesight and can give early warning of danger.

▼ Mountain zebras from South Africa.

▲ The Grevy's zebra can be recognized by its huge ears and narrowly spaced stripes.

There are three kinds of zebra living in Africa today. But there was once a fourth. The quagga had brown and white stripes on its neck and head and a brown body. There were once millions of these animals, but they were hunted so heavily that by 1861 there were none left.

Duck-billed Platypus

POISONOUS EGG-LAYER

Mammals, from mice to humans, usually give birth to live young and feed the young with their own milk. Reptiles and birds usually lay eggs. The duck-billed platypus, however, is very unusual because it is a mammal that lays eggs.

At breeding time, the adult platypuses make a special nesting burrow in the bank of a river. They dig the soil with the broad nails on their front feet. The burrow may be 30 m long with one or more nesting chambers.

The female lays two or three soft-shelled eggs, which hatch after ten days. From then on, they behave much more like mammals: the young feed on the mother's milk until they are old enough to leave the burrow.

▲ Duck-billed platypuses are carnivorous – they eat insects and other small animals that live on the bottom of fresh-water streams and rivers. Under water, a platypus closes its eyes and uses its soft and sensitive beak to feel for food in the mud.

▼ Platypuses are good swimmers. They paddle with their webbed front feet, using their back feet to steer.

The duck-billed platypus is one of the very few mammals to use venom as a way of defending itself. The male has a hollow spur on the back of his ankle and delivers the venom with a forceful jab of his back legs.

Kangaroo

POUCHED HOPPERS

With their powerful back legs and huge feet, kangaroos are probably the best 'hoppers' in the world. The largest kind, the grey kangaroo, is 2 m tall and can jump as high off the ground. It can leap distances of 8 m at speeds of 40 kph, though some people say they have seen them jump higher and faster than this.

Like many Australian animals, the kangaroo is a marsupial. The young are born very small and grow inside a pouch on the mother's body. New-born grey kangaroos are less than 25 mm long. They crawl through their mothers' fur to the pouch and begin to feed on milk from one of the teats they find there.

▲ A male red kangaroo hopping. When it jumps, the kangaroo holds its long tail out behind it to act as a counter-balance.

▼ A grey kangaroo and her joey. After about two months, the joey will venture out of its mother's pouch in search of food. After nine months, it will leave the pouch altogether.

There is no real difference between a kangaroo and a wallaby. Traditionally, wallabies are smaller than kangaroos.

Opossum

ANIMAL THAT PLAYS DEAD

Marsupials are animals which give birth to tiny young that then develop inside a pouch on the mother's body. Most marsupials live in Australia and its neighbouring islands. Opossums are unusual because they are marsupials that live in North and South America.

The best known is the Virginia opossum. It feeds at night on the ground, but can take to the trees if alarmed and climbs well. Young ones

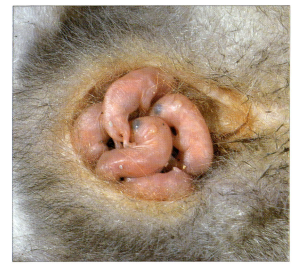

▲ A family of opossums in their mother's pouch. They are only a few days old.

After leaving their mother's pouch, baby opossums cling to her back while she forages for food. She may have so many babies on board that she can hardly walk.

can curl their tails around branches and dangle upside down. At birth, opossum babies crawl through the mother's fur and into her pouch. She has enough teats in the pouch to feed thirteen babies.

An opossum that is chased by a dog or a coyote, will growl and hiss, but if it is seized it will play dead. Its body goes completely limp. Many predators will then lose interest, for they will not eat animals that are already dead.

◄ On their back feet, opossums have an opposable toe. This means that it can be folded across the sole of the foot, just as our thumb folds across our palm. This helps the animal to get a good grip on branches.

Aye-aye

LONG-FINGERED PROBER

The aye-aye is unlike any other kind of animal. It is related to the lemurs, but is really in a family of its own (the Daubentonidae) because of its unique appearance and habits. The aye-aye is found only on the island of Madagascar off the coast of south-eastern Africa.

The aye-aye sleeps during the day in a nest. At night it ventures out to feed on fruit and young insects, or larvae, clinging to the branches with its long claws. With its very strong teeth, the aye-aye is able to break the hard outer shells of fruits, such as coconuts.

The aye-aye catches insect larvae with its middle finger, which is long and thin and has an extra long claw. It pushes its finger into holes, skewers the larvae and carries them to its mouth.

▲ A young aye-aye climbing a tree in the rainforests of Madagascar.

The aye-aye is an odd-looking animal. Many of the people of Madagascar, the Malagasy, think that the aye-aye brings them bad luck. If they see one, they kill it immediately. It is also in danger of becoming extinct because its rainforest home is being chopped down.

▼ An aye-aye devouring an egg. It is scraping the contents out of the shell with its long third finger.

Gibbon

SWINGING SINGER

Of all the apes, the gibbons are the champions of swing. With their long arms, they can propel themselves through the forests of south-eastern Asia, swinging from branch to branch, with great agility and speed. They can swing a distance of 9 m easily.

Gibbons live in family groups made up of a male and female and their offspring. Each group has its own area of forest, the individuals spending much of their time cleaning, or grooming, each other and picking fruit with their long, supple fingers.

The forest rings with their songs. The most spectacular song of all comes from

▲ Female gibbons carry their young with them. This white-cheeked gibbon is carrying her 30-day old baby.

the female Kloss gibbon. She sings for two hours after dawn, a series of rising and falling notes. At the climax of her song, she trills loudly, and may run up and down branches, breaking off leaves. Her call tells other females nearby to keep away from her mate.

In some gibbons, the male and female strengthen the bond between them by singing duets which last for about fifteen minutes.

◀ Siamangs are the largest species of gibbon; they live on the islands of Sumatra and Malacca. This one is making its territorial call using its large throat sac. The air is exhaled with a shriek.

Gorilla

GENTLE GIANT

Gorillas look scary with their gruff faces and great size, but in fact they are peaceful vegetarians. They spend most of their time chewing leaves and stems, wandering about their African forest homes or just sleeping.

There are three races of gorillas: the eastern lowland, the western lowland and the mountain. Mountain gorillas live in a very small area in central Africa, in the Virunga mountains. They have long, thick hair to help them stay warm. The

▲ A group of young mountain gorillas – they are our closest relatives in the animal world. Fossils, and a new understanding of how their bodies work, have shown that they are closer to humans than to orang-utans.

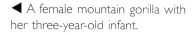

◀ A female mountain gorilla with her three-year-old infant.

gorillas live in groups which are led by an adult male, the silverback.

Each group is made up of several females and their young. The silverback leads them to food, and at night he selects a place for them all to rest. They bend over branches to make nests in which to sleep. The silverback keeps other males away with a frightening display of hoots and chest-beats.

There are very few mountain gorillas left in the wild, perhaps just over 300. They are protected in a national park which is patrolled by armed guards. Poachers still hunt them for their skins and skulls, and endanger the gorillas' lives by laying traps for other animals in which the gorillas may be caught accidentally.

Japanese Macaques

MONKEYS IN THE SNOW

Japanese macaques live further north than any other kind of monkey. They can be found in mountain forests and rocky hillsides, which are often thick with snow in winter, so these monkeys have thick shaggy coats. Japanese macaques form troops of 20–200 individuals. They eat fruit, insects, young leaves and small animals.

One group, studied by scientists, ate large numbers of sweet potatoes. They lived by the coast. One day, a female discovered that her potato tasted better if she washed it. This behaviour quickly spread throughout the group. Later they discovered that they could separate grains of rice from sand by throwing it into the water (the rice floated).

▲ There is a very strong bond between a female macaque and her infant, which may last for life.

▼ In the cold Japanese winters, macaques keep warm by bathing in hot springs. The water is heated deep in the ground and rises to form steaming pools.

Macaques often share their home ranges with other monkeys called langurs. The two are able to live in the same parts of the forest because they do not compete for food. Langurs eat only leaves.

Proboscis Monkey

BIG HOOTERS

Proboscis monkeys live in the hot wet forests and mangrove swamps of Borneo and southern China. They spend the day in the swamps and return to higher trees to sleep. They move about by swinging through the branches They can also swim well and will drop 15 m into a stream in order to cross it.

They live in troops of up to sixty and seem to get along without the chattering and fighting common in other monkey groups. Each troop has its own home range in the centre of which are the trees in which they sleep. The boss-male will warn other troops of their position with whooping noises.

The male's big nose, which overhangs the mouth in older monkeys, straightens out when he makes his honking alarm call. It seems that the strange shape of the nose helps to make the call louder.

▲ Proboscis monkeys are leaf-eaters. They live in swampy forests and rest at night in tall pedada trees.

Each troop may have males and females, or just males, but there is always one dominant (or 'boss') male. He may sometimes bite, but will also groom the other members. A proboscis monkey mother will allow other females to look after her young. One female will sometimes babysit for several youngsters. This is unusual behaviour among animals.

▼ The nose of the proboscis monkey is unmistakable.

Tarsier

BIG-EYED LEAPERS

These strange little animals live in the forests of islands in south-east Asia. They live in the trees, spending much of their time clinging to upright trunks. Tarsiers can shuffle awkwardly along branches, but usually get about by jumping. They straighten their long back legs suddenly and leap into the air, turning in mid-leap if necessary, to land on another tree up to 2 m away.

With their large eyes, tarsiers are well-adapted to hunting at night. They eat insects, frogs, lizards and birds. One species is known to catch and eat birds larger than themselves and also poisonous snakes.

Young tarsiers are born very advanced. They have thick fur and their eyes are open. As soon as they are born, they can climb and cling to their mother's fur. If she is travelling long distances, she carries the young one in her mouth.

▲ A tarsier can turn its head almost right around without moving the rest of its body. This helps it to see its prey and avoid predators, such as owls and small cats.

Like many other animals that are active at night, the tarsier has large eyes. In fact, at 3 grams in weight, each eye is heavier than the animal's brain. They are always alert for danger. Even when resting, a tarsier will keep one eye open.

◄ Tarsiers have long fingers and toes. Each one has a sucker-like disc-pad at the tip and these help the animal to grip on to tree trunks and branches.

Animal Jumbles

Find the letters that go in the circles. The circled letters make 3-, 4-, 5- and 6-letter words with the letters written beside them. For example,

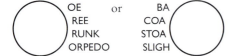

OE
REE
RUNK
ORPEDO

or

BA
COA
STOA
SLIGH

would give you the letter T in the circle. (Toe, Tree, Trunk, Torpedo; or Bat, Coat, Stoat, Slight). When you have found all the circled letters, rearrange them to make the words for different groups of animals.

1

OA
ARB
LOOD
OBCAT

HY
ALT
PEED
CARAB

PO
WOO
APHI
LIZAR

TS
BEX
NDIA
GUANA

EA
YEA
BOWE
WEAVE

Answer: ◯ ◯ ◯ ◯ ◯

Clue: Most of these animals can fly.

2

OX
ROG
ATAL
ENNEC

LL
BIS
VORY
NSECT

ZO
SOL
GECK
POTAT

AN
OSS
AMBA
ANTIS

OW
TOO
SMEL
TUNNE

Answer: ◯ ◯ ◯
◯ ◯ ◯ ◯ ◯ ◯

Clue: The hunting dog belongs to this group.

DI
SON
STIN
ZIGZA

AM
IET
IVER
RAGON

DA
BON
SALT
COLON

IR
SIA
NDES
YEAYE

3

RB
NLY
RGAN
UNCES

OD
UKU
ANDA
UPATE

EX
EED
ATIN
ALIVA

IT
IWI
LOSS
OMODO

AC
TAG
KUNK
PIDER

FL
BOD
IVOR
WOOLL

SE
MAL
MOOS
MALLE

BO
GIL
COBR
BROLG

UD
ALE
IMIC
OLOCH

SU
SKI
ACOR
POLLE

BE
BIT
GRAZ
BEETL

Answer: ◯ ◯ ◯ ◯ and
◯ ◯ ◯ ◯ ◯ ◯

Clue: Our closest relatives in the animal world.

Answers can be found on page 111

Index

109

Picture Acknowledgements

t=top, b=below

Oxford Scientific Films: 19t, 24t: Doug Allan 61b; Kathie Atkinson 25b, 39b; Anthony Bannister 44b; Eyal Bartov 81t, 89b, 95t; George I. Bernard 11b, 15t, 23t, 27t; Mike Birkhead 49b; Derek Bromhall 63t; Clive Bromhall 107t; Roger Brown 55t; David Cayless cover & 86t; Martyn Colbeck cover & 87t; Peter Cook 42t, 65b; J.A.L. Cooke 28bl, 29t, 29b; John Cooke 99t; Rob Cousins 96b; Daniel J. Cox 79t; David Curl cover & 43b; Irvine Cushing 21t; Bruce Davidson 80t, 104t; Richard Davies 17t; Tui de Roy 45b, 60t, 61t; Mark Deeble & Victoria Stone 93b; Stephen Downer cover & 36b; Paolo Fioratti 63b; David B. Fleetham

30b; Michael Fogden 21b, cover & 31b, 32b, 40t, 44t, 96t; Joaquin Gutierrez Acha 26t, 26b; Mark Hamblin 49t; F. David Haring 102b; Geoff Higgins cover & 14b; Mike Hill 9t; Mark Jones cover & 45t; Michael Leach 14t, 35b, cover & 58t; Ted Levin 59b; David MacDonald cover & 72t, 72b; Alastair MacEwen 33b; John Mitchell 9b; Muzz Murray 58b; Owen Newma 68t; Lloyd Nielsen 47; Stan Oslinski 56, 10, 38t, 90t; Peter Parks cover & 11t; Partridge Productions Ltd 106t; Michael Pitts 38b; Dieter & Mary Plage 18t, 18b; Andrew Plumptree cover & 104b; Avril Ramage 15b; Robin Redfern 83b; J.H. Robinson 35t; Alan Root 37b; Norbert Rosing 48t, 64t, 97t; Alastair Shay 19b; Jorge Sierra Antinolo 48b; Claude Steelman 73b; Harold Taylow 13b; David Thompson 24b, 25t; Robert A. Tyrrell 53t, 6 & 53b; Tom Ulrich 34t, 36t, 76t, 101b;

P. & W. Ward 28t, 71t, 71b; Babs & Bert Wells 43t; Konrad Wothe 62t, 7 & 78, 102t; Belinda Wright 39t.
Animals Animals: Jerry Cooke 7 & 106b; Dr. E.R. Degginger 82t; Michael Dick 103t; Esao Hashimoto 105t; Breck P. Kent 83b, 101t; Richard K. La Val 28br; Zig Leszczynski 31t, 33t, 41b, 92b; Joe McDonald cover & 37t; Raymond A. Mendez 8; Brian Milne 90b; Peter Weimann 77t.
Dinodia Picture Agency: Jagdish Agarwal 84t; Isaac Kehimkar 27b.
Photo Researchers: Ron Austing 92t; Mark N. Boulton 75t; Scott Camazine 73t; Alan D. Carey 6 & 88t; Gregory G. Dimijian 70b; Dan Guravich 20b; George Holton 86b; Renee Lynn 76b; Tom McHugh cover & 42t; 46t, 46b, 52b, 54, 67b, 69t, cover & 69b, 99, 107b; Rod Planck cover & 74t; Harry

Rogers 23b; Jany Sauvanet 67t; R. Van Nostrand 81b, 103b.
Survival Anglia: Andrew Anerson 59t; Des & Jean Bartless 55b, cover & 57b, 57t, 82b, 87b, 88b, 95b, 98b, 100b, 100t; Joel Bennett 91t, 91b, 105t; Liz & Tony Bomford 65t; Frances Furlong 12t, 12b, 16t; John Harris cover & 41t; Nick Gordon cover, 1 & 98t; Dennis Green cover & 20t; Peter Hawkey 64b; Richard & Julia Kemp 62b; Dr. F. Köster 34b; Keith & Liz Laidler 66t; Mike Linley 16b, 32t, 40b; Andrew Park 69t; William Paton 93t; Malcolm Penny 77b; Dieter & Mary Plage 22, 6 & 30t, 50t, 50b, cover & 51t, 51b, 68b, 85; Mary Plage cover & 79b, cover & 70t; Mike Price 74b; Purdy & Matthews 80b, 97b; Alan Root 17b, 52t, 66b, 75b, 94t, 94b; Vivek Sinha 60b, 84t; Claude Steelman 13t; Michael Strobino 89t.